RICE PAPER MEMOIRS

片紙札記 － 憶往情懷

Joy Lee Han

BIRCHVIEW PRESS

Milwaukee

ISBN: 978-0-692-98520-5
Library of Congress Control Number: 2017960650

Photographs in the background on pages xiv, 6, 12, 18, 24, 28, 44, 50, 56, 62, 70, 84, 90, 112, and 122 are public domain images from Wikimedia. Photograph on page 67 provided courtesy of the University of Mary Hardin-Baylor. All other images belong to the author.

Cover: Background images are taken from the author's 1946 journal entries written on rice paper. The image on the front cover describes arriving late for church after a heavy rain; the image on the back cover recounts nighttime gunfire and fear of a Communist attack. The front cover photo is from the author's first passport in 1947.

Book production: Kate Hawley by Design, Milwaukee, Wisconsin

Published by:

BIRCHVIEW PRESS
Milwaukee, Wisconsin
www.birchviewpress.com
birchviewpress@gmail.com

I wish to dedicate this book to
all who walk in faith
and to the memory of
my parents, Dr. and Mrs. Peter Lee,
and my mentor, Miss Zemma Hare.

TABLE OF CONTENTS

目錄

FOREWORD

前言

Though we may know the course of history, it is the stories of people caught up in its events that capture our interest. This memoir by my mother, Joy Lee Han, is such a story. From tumultuous times in mainland China to a rural existence in the peaceful Upper Peninsula of Michigan, events both titanic and ephemeral affected a young Chinese girl and her family in ways unimaginable to most people. Some of these events were geopolitical and violent, including the Japanese invasion of China, conflicts between Chinese Communist and Nationalist regimes, and World War II. Yet, episodes such as my grandmother's finger infection, which brought her and her future family under the fold of Western missionaries, and the decisive prodding of a stranger to illicitly cross the border from Communist China into Hong Kong were as powerful as any news headline of the day.

The story of Joy, an immigrant to the United States from revolutionary China, and those of others like her, are not familiar to most Americans. This is not surprising, given the powerful narratives that describe the American experience in the European and Pacific theaters in World War II—records of tremendous sacrifice that profoundly reshaped the world. Yet these narratives fail to capture the stories of my parents, Tsu-Ming and Joy, whose experiences occurred even farther away in the interior of China. As their son, a Chinese American boy growing up in the Upper Peninsula of Michigan in the 1960s and '70s, I heard their individual tales of turmoil; these experiences had occurred in a mother country alien to me, but were firmly connected to world events. I believed that their stories needed to be told. Their friends, many from the Upper Peninsula, and of Scandinavian and Northern European descent, agreed.

The river of life that is Joy's experience begins calmly at her South Tree Pavilion, an idyllic place of peace and friendship. But this calmness belied the imminent cascade of war, political upheaval, pulmonary tuberculosis, and a struggle to reunite with emigrant family members in the United States. Who would believe that a large American flag painted on your roof to avoid bombing would, in a moment, turn your living area from a protectorate to a military target? Forces beyond my mother's control, many affecting the entire world, led to a far different existence than most of her peers would experience. The remarkable guidance of relatives, friends, and strangers, as well as Joy's extraordinary faith, brought her to a place where the river of life ran smooth, but where the turbulence upstream continued to exert its influence through a childhood acquaintance and lingering symptoms of lung disease long ago healed.

Why did Joy eventually set roots in the Upper Peninsula of Michigan? This question is relevant because her history adds to the diverse experiences of many immigrants and minorities who settled there. The Upper Peninsula is the site of the confluence of two timeless endeavors: mining and human migration. Miners were among the first Chinese immigrants to the United States, drawn by the California gold rush in the mid-1800s. And although the first Chinese to arrive in Upper Michigan were laundrymen and restaurateurs, it was the mining industry that drew them there. A century later, it was mining that brought Joy and Tsu-Ming to the small Upper Peninsula town of Ishpeming. There, as a research scientist working for what was then called the Cleveland-Cliffs Iron Company, Tsu-Ming would make significant contributions to Michigan's iron industry. Joy was at his side, melding her own cultural background with those of Finns, Swedes, and Norwegians. She is the only person I know who can speak Mandarin, English, and many words of Finnish.

As one of Joy's children, I am but a mere footnote to her story. My challenge was being brought up by parents uninformed about Western culture and social norms. This was a trifle in the grand scheme of things. Joy's memoir tells an astoundingly different story. I realized just how different when she casually mentioned, as we watched the film *The Book Thief* together, that the scenes showing frightened German families sheltering themselves from Allied bombs revived her own childhood memories of huddling in basements while being bombed by the Japanese.

My mother's story is a saga of an abundant life made possible through great providence and the incredible kindnesses of friends and strangers in China and America, a journey that eventually led her to become a full-fledged American who takes not one shred of her freedoms for granted. It is also a reminder that most Americans, myself included, should be profoundly grateful for one of the greatest privileges of all time: being a citizen of the United States of America.

—Dennis P. Han

PREFACE

序言

I wrote this book at the encouragement of friends and family. It is the story of my life, which I wish to share with my loved ones and anyone else who is interested in the history of China and its people. It is also a story of faith and determination, two things that have shaped and guided my life from the beginning, and which I hope will inspire those who read this memoir. I am proud of my Chinese heritage and culture, but also have come to dearly love my adopted country and my home of more than sixty years, the city of Ishpeming, in the Upper Peninsula of Michigan. I hope my story adds to the history of this extraordinary place.

I would like to acknowledge the people who helped me write this memoir. My editor, Priscilla Pardini, worked with me to organize the material and smooth out my writing. Kate Hawley did a beautiful job designing the book's pages and cover. My dear, longtime friend Marie Rogers continually urged me to finish this book! And my brother, Joseph Lee, graciously provided the Chinese translations and some of the photographs that added so much to this project. Last but not least, I am indebted to my three children: Dennis, who found the right people to bring this book to fruition and helped coordinate their efforts and mine, along with Tim and Lisa, who stood by me with patience and encouragement throughout the past three years as I struggled to continue. To all, I extend my most sincere and heartfelt thanks!

—Joy Lee Han

JOY LEE HAN'S CHINA

地圖

Yellow River

Beijing

Kaifeng

Luoyang
Zhengzhou

Xi'an

Suzhou Shanghai

Guangzhou

Hong Kong

Tokyo

A BRIEF CHRONOLOGY OF THE EVENTS THAT SHAPED THE WORLD AND LIFE OF JOY LEE HAN

年表

1636   The Qing dynasty, the last imperial dynasty of China, is established.

1800s   The first Protestant missionaries arrive in China in 1807; Southern Baptist Convention missionaries from the United States arrive in the 1830s; missionaries from the non-sectarian China Inland Mission arrive in 1866.

1882   The US Chinese Exclusion Act, the only federal law to prohibit the immigration of a specific nationality of people, is enacted. The law is passed in response to growing anti-immigrant sentiment by Americans in the western United States.

1911   The Qing dynasty comes to an end and is replaced by the Republic of China.

1930   Joy is born in Kaifeng, Henan Province, China, on October 29. Joy resides at and attends school in the Baptist Compound run by the US-based Southern Baptist missionaries until 1941.

1937– 1945   China and Japan are continuously at war. Chinese Nationalists and Communists form an alliance to resist.

1941   The Japanese attack Pearl Harbor on December 8, bringing the United States into World War II. The Baptist Compound in Kaifeng is occupied by Japanese forces and Joy and her family are forced to flee.

1943   The US Chinese Exclusion Act of 1882 is repealed.

1947   Joy is denied passage to the United States to attend college due to evidence of tuberculosis detected on a screening chest x-ray.

1948   Joy, her mother, sister, and four brothers arrive in Shanghai in December.

1949   On her way to Los Angeles in May, Joy's sister, Lois Lee, takes the last plane out of Shanghai to Hong Kong. Six days later, Joy witnesses Shanghai's fall to the Communists as Nationalist Chinese leaders flee to Taiwan. Officially sanctioned immigration to the United States is suspended. Communication between Peter Lee in the United States and his family in China is cut off.

1950   Joy emigrates to the United States via Hong Kong in October after making an illicit border crossing between China and the Kowloon Peninsula. She arrives in San Francisco on November 4, and then is admitted to the Oakville Memorial Sanatorium in Memphis, Tennessee, for treatment of tuberculosis. Joy remains there until the summer of 1952.

1950–1953 North Korea invades South Korea, starting the Korean War. United Nations forces, made up primarily of Americans, come to the assistance of South Korea while Chinese "volunteers" join the war on the North Korean side.

1952 Joy enrolls at Mary Hardin-Baylor College, in Belton, Texas, where she receives outpatient treatment for tuberculosis at Scott and White Hospital in Temple, Texas, for one year.

1953 Joy's mother, Ruth Lee, and Joy's brothers, Samuel, Joseph, Eugene, and James, arrive in the United States in January.

1955 Joy completes the required coursework for a BS in biology. One year later she completes an internship at Saginaw General Hospital in Saginaw, Michigan, receives her degree, and is certified as a medical technologist.

1956 In Washington, DC, Joy marries Tsu-Ming Han, a PhD candidate in geology at the University of Minnesota in Minneapolis, in July. Their children are born in 1957, 1958, and 1962.

1956 The era of McCarthyism, a fear of Communist infiltration of the American political system also known as "the second Red Scare," comes to an end in the United States, but not before the FBI investigates Joy's husband, Tsu-Ming Han, for nonexistent Communist connections.

1962 Joy obtains American citizenship on December 4.

1966–1976 The Cultural Revolution, a movement seeking to solidify Communist ideology at the expense of capitalism and traditional Chinese values, takes place in China.

1979 The United States and the People's Republic of China establish diplomatic relations. Joy, her parents, and her brother Joseph visit relatives in China they had not seen or heard from in almost thirty years.

1980s–1990s Christian churches in China are re-established.

1985 Joy's father, Peter Lee, dies.

1999–present Joy's daughter, Lisa, resides in Xi'an, China.

2005 Joy's husband, Tsu-Ming Han, dies.

2008 Joy's mother, Ruth Lee, dies.

EDITOR'S NOTE

Chinese terms and most proper names are printed in the Pinyin convention. Exceptions are made when the Wade-Giles spelling is well known and more likely to be familiar to the reader.

编者之言

Chapter 1

MY CHINESE ANCESTORS

The earliest memory I have is of my grandmother. She was my father's mother and lived with us for as long as I can remember. Her name was Li Yangrong (李楊榮) and she was born in 1867, during the Qing dynasty, in a little village called Kwotien located south of the city of Kaifeng in Henan Province in north central China. She had given birth to two daughters before my father was born. Later in her life, when she was a widow, she was referred to as Lady Li Yang, but we called her Nai-Nai.

My grandmother was short and quite slender. As a child, her feet had been bound, which was traditional for girls at the time. By the time I knew her, she wore her graying hair in a bun on the back of her head, a style that was customary for older, married women in China. She was the matriarch of our household and was feared and respected by family members and servants alike. My grandmother often took me with her to visit her friends, or to the local railroad station where we watched trains speeding by. I always wondered where they were going, and wished

that someday I would be able to ride the train to faraway places. My paternal grandfather had been a farmer named Li Yongcheng (李永誠), who was determined that his son, my father, would grow up to live an honorable life working the fields.

My father's given name was Li Xingxian (李興賢), which means "propagating virtue." He was born in 1905 in Kwotien. When he was about nine years old, my father was given his first job: to go out into the fields to chase birds and other animals away from the crops. My father, however, wanted to go to the village school. Although my grandfather objected, my father was determined. He would go out into the fields, but refused to eat until my grandfather changed his mind.

The first school my father attended was in Kwotien, and it emphasized classic Chinese works of literature and a few other subjects. Students were required to memorize long passages from the classics and recite them verbatim standing in front of the teacher's desk facing the class. My father did this very well, learned quickly, and was promoted to more and

我的華夏家世

Opposite foreground: My paternal grandmother, Li Yangrong, whom I called Nai-Nai, looks stern in this photo, but we spent a lot of time together when I was growing up and were very close.

Opposite background: Kaifeng, my hometown, was a bustling city in 1910. The banner hanging over this street in the city's Eastern Market is advertising a local tea shop. The rickshaws, still popular when I was growing up, were a way for us to travel around the city.

1

more advanced classes. After about four years he persuaded his parents to send him to another school that had been started by Christian missionaries from the United States who were affiliated with the Southern Baptist Convention. The school was located in a big mansion in Kwotien. It had been built during the Qing dynasty as a place for emperors and other important officials and their entourages to stay on their way from the capital city, Beijing, to the south of China on pleasure trips. At the time, the building was known as the Royal Hotel. However, when the Qing dynasty—the last imperial dynasty—was overturned by the establishment of the Republic of China in 1911, the mansion fell into disuse and started to deteriorate. A story went around that it was inhabited by ghosts whose heads were seen rolling around on the floor. The mansion became known as the Haunted House, and nobody dared to go in. When the missionaries offered to buy the building, the local people were very happy to sell it to them. It was here that my father first encountered Christianity. He was baptized at the age of thirteen, and soon after that converted his parents to Christianity.

At that point, my father moved from his village to the city of Kaifeng, almost a day's journey northwest, to continue his education at the Boys' School located in a large compound run by the Southern Baptist missionaries. At the compound, which was several miles south of Kaifeng and surrounded by farmland, there were separate schools for boys and girls, and homes for the Baptist missionaries who worked there. On the main floor of the Girls' School was an auditorium that doubled

My father, whose Christian name was Peter H. Lee, was a student at the University of Shanghai in the early 1930s.

as a church. My father got a job milking the missionaries' cows to subsidize the cost of his tuition. One day while he was in high school, my father was called home because his father was dying. His family took comfort in the fact that because of his Christian faith, his death was peaceful. My father returned to Kaifeng, graduated from high school with honors, and then enrolled at what was then the University of Shanghai. It had been established by the American Baptist Missionary Union and the Southern Baptist Convention, and was ranked as one of the best Christian schools in China. After studying for two years at the university, he was called back to Kaifeng to teach at the Boys' School in the Baptist Compound.

My mother's maiden name was Niu Caiqin (牛彩勤), meaning "acquire diligence," but her Christian name—given to her many years later by her good friend Miss Zemma Hare, an American missionary—was Ruth. My mother was born in Kaifeng, in 1905, to a devout Buddhist family. She was the third of three girls, which was a great disappointment to her parents because, of course, in China boys were preferred. This feeling of disappointment was even stronger in 1903 than when I was born twenty-seven years later.

My mother did not remember her father, who died when she was only two years old, leaving the family financially destitute. Her mother, whom we called Lao-Lao, took in sewing for people and performed other odd jobs to make a living. She was quiet and reserved, and a strict Buddhist. As a child, her feet had been tightly bound, but she gave my mother permission to bind her own feet,

My mother, Niu Caiqin, whose Christian name was Ruth, became a kindergarten teacher.

We called my maternal grandmother (right) Lao-Lao. Here she is with one of my mother's sisters, having tea.

one of them. This was her earnest desire for many years. However, my mother's oldest sister married young and had several children, and my mother helped take care of them. For a while, my mother thought caring for her nieces and nephews would be her life's calling and that she would never get married. Her second sister married a merchant and died young, without children.

One day when my mother was about fourteen years old, she was helping with the sewing when she pricked her finger with a needle. Her finger became infected and she went to a Chinese doctor. When it did not get better, he told her that the finger must be amputated. My mother did not like that idea, so my grandmother sent her to a nearby clinic operated by the Baptist Church. At the clinic, a "Bible woman," as the women ministry workers were called, looked at my mother's finger and sterilized a needle with alcohol. She opened up the wound with the needle, squeezed out the pus, and then applied some medicine and bandaged the finger up. My mother was told to come back after a few days.

Because my mother could not do any sewing while her finger was infected, my grandmother told her she might as well go to school to learn something useful.

which she did loosely, allowing her feet to grow somewhat. When my mother was very young, she accompanied her mother to the Buddhist temple to worship and burn incense. She observed the nuns and the serenity of their demeanor and appearance when they proceeded to the temple and knelt down to worship, and thought that she would like to become

The missionaries who ran the clinic also operated a grade school, where my mother started attending classes. In the meantime, her finger completely healed. She was older and bigger than the other pupils, but she did not mind. She learned very quickly and within three years advanced to the sixth grade. After sixth grade, she was sent to the Baptist Compound to attend junior high, which is where she met Miss Zemma Hare, principal of the Girls' School. Even though my mother never finished high school, Miss Hare hired her to teach kindergarten at the Girls' School in the compound.

When I was about seven years old, Lao-Lao—who had lived with us for a while, but whom I don't remember very well—died. Her death was the first I had ever experienced, and I remember that her casket was kept for a short time in a room in our house. One of the rituals of death in our area was for the eldest daughter to dip a piece of cotton in a bowl of water, use the cotton to wipe the face of the deceased, and then drink the water to show filial piety. I remember my aunt doing this. I also remember that I was lifted up to look upon the face of my grandmother as a way to pay my respects. The next day, an oxcart and driver were hired to carry my grandmother's casket to the cemetery. We, the mourners, followed in another oxcart. The color of death was white, and all the mourners wore white sackcloth over their clothing and sewed a piece of white cloth onto the front of each of their shoes. When people walking down the streets saw the funeral procession, they would stop, either out of curiosity or respect.

Chapter 2

A FIRSTBORN CHILD

It was Miss Hare who introduced my parents. Even though my mother and father had both gone to school—and taught—in the Baptist Compound, the Boys' and Girls' Schools were completely separated, and they did not know each other. They met for the first time in Miss Hare's home when they were in their twenties. By then, both my parents had converted to the Christian faith, and the missionaries had given my father the Christian name Peter, and changed his surname from Li to Lee. Soon after meeting, my parents became engaged. They were married on April 26, 1927, at the chapel of the Kaifeng Baptist College, by an American missionary, Dr. W. Eugene Sallee.

Because my parents were both teachers in the Baptist Compound, they were given a house there after they were married. But soon, with my mother's encouragement, my father returned to the University of Shanghai to continue his education while she stayed behind teaching and looking after her mother and mother-in-law.

I was born on October 29, 1930, the firstborn of my parents' seven children. For many years I thought I had been born in the China Inland Mission Hospital outside of Kaifeng, a hospital established by missionaries from England. But my mother told me later that I was born in an upstairs room of a church building near the Drum Tower, a landmark in central Kaifeng, and that she and I were only taken to the hospital afterward. I was given the name Meirui, which means "beautiful luck." Chinese names usually consist of three syllables, with the first syllable being the family name. Thus, my Chinese name is Li Meirui (李美瑞). My English name, Joy, was given to me by Miss Hare. My father was at the University of Shanghai when I was born, earning his bachelor of arts degree with a major in education later that year. He then worked as principal of a high school in Shanghai before moving back home.

After me there came six siblings. My sister Lois was born nearly two years after me, and then came another girl who died in infancy of whooping cough. Four boys

頭生的孩子

Opposite foreground: My mother rode a donkey to my father's village after their wedding in 1927.

Opposite background: Shanghai in the 1920s and 1930s, when my father attended college there, was already a big, bustling city.

7

Left: When I was born in 1930 I was named Li Meirui, meaning "beautiful luck." Here I am with my grandmother, Nai-Nai.

Right: My Christian name, given to me by an American Baptist missionary was Joy. Here I am with my mother.

followed. Their names, in the order of their birth, were Samuel, Joseph, Eugene, and James. I remember my grandmother saying something like this to her friends: "I was really disappointed when the third girl came, but she was such a beautiful baby that I loved her just the same." When I was old enough to understand things, I wished I had been born a boy. How wonderful it would have been if I, the firstborn, were a boy! No one ever made me feel that way, but knowing boys were more treasured than girls in Chinese culture, and remembering my grandmother's comment, I felt I might have been a disappointment to my family.

My hometown, the city of Kaifeng, is located about six miles south of the Yellow River, which was known as "China's Sorrow" because it often overflowed its banks, destroying land and people. In ancient times the city was called Bianjing. Kaifeng served as the capital city of China during the Northern Song dynasty, which lasted from 960 to 1127, a period of Chinese military might that is said to have included the formation of the first official standing navy in the world. Poetry and literature flourished during this dynasty (the famous lady poet Li Qingzhao lived then, composing many poems and verses), as did painting and the performing arts. Inventions included the magnetic compass and moveable type, which enabled the printing of large quantities of books. Gunpowder was used for the first time, not only for warfare but also for fireworks.

Kaifeng was the largest city in the world from 1013 to 1127, and had a population of between six and seven hundred thousand people. In the northeastern corner of the city, there was a settlement of families of Jewish descent whose ancestors had begun migrating to China over the Silk Road from Persia or India as early as the Tang dynasty (618–907). Arriving either overland or by a sea route, their numbers grew, and in 1163 they built a synagogue in Kaifeng. During the Ming dynasty (1368–1644), an emperor conferred seven surnames upon the Jews, by which they are still identified today: Ai, Shi, Gao, Jin, Li, Zhang, and Zhao. Three stelae, stone slabs featuring commemorative inscriptions about the Jewish community, were found in Kaifeng. The oldest is thought to date back to 1489. Interestingly, a book written by Pearl S. Buck, *Peony*, is about a Jewish family living in Kaifeng in the 1850s that had a young, Chinese maid who grew up with their only son, David.

The city of Kaifeng was once surrounded by a high, thick wall that had a gate on each of its four sides. There were

watchtowers on top of the wall at certain intervals. Remnants of that ancient wall and a few of the many ancient temples and pagodas that had been located within Kaifeng were still in place when I was growing up, and remain in place today. A palace called the Dragon Pavilion (formerly the Dragon *Throne*) is situated at a high point in the city just inside of what's left of the northern wall. The road leading to the Dragon Pavilion is approximately a mile long, with a lake on either side. It was said that one lake had clear water and the other muddy, symbolizing two Song dynasty generals: one loyal to, and one a traitor to, the dynasty. According

My sister, Lois (right), and I were less than two years apart in age and spent a lot of time together growing up. Here we are with our mother in 1934.

The Dragon Pavilion (top) is part of the Song imperial palace, and the Iron Pagoda (bottom) is part of the Youguo Temple. Both were built about nine hundred years ago during the Song dynasty, in my hometown of Kaifeng.

to legend, a giant bronze bell with treasures hidden beneath it rests at the bottom of one of the lakes. By the time I was a child, the area around the Dragon Pavilion had become a public park where families would go for outings or picnics. One had to climb many steps to reach the open area of the pavilion and enter the

throne room, from which the emperor ruled during the Northern Song dynasty. It was worth the effort to make the climb because when standing on the top step you had a clear view straight down a wide avenue toward the south city gate.

A short distance to the east stood the Iron Pagoda, first built in 989, but destroyed by fire in 1044 and rebuilt in 1049. In China, pagodas have an odd number of levels. The Iron Pagoda, the highest structure in Kaifeng, had thirteen, with a stairway that gradually got narrower and narrower the higher it went. On each level, there was a little window to look out of, and from the top nearly the whole city could be seen. As a child, I was taken by my parents to climb the Iron Pagoda, but had been afraid to go higher than the fourth level.

In the center of the city was the Drum Tower, which had been built with an arch through which people and vehicles could pass. On the south side of the tower was a narrow street that once led to the prime minister's monastery. The monastery's main building was a Buddhist temple surrounded by smaller buildings, perhaps the dwelling places of monks and servants. After the end of the last imperial Chinese dynasty in 1911, this area became a very busy and popular bazaar

for trading and acrobatic performances. I remember my parents taking us there frequently and buying us cotton candy. Kaifeng was quite a busy city when I was growing up, and because there were no motorized vehicles we often rode in rickshaws to get from place to place when it was too far to walk. The two-wheeled rickshaws were everywhere, and pulling the rickshaws was one way that men in Kaifeng earned money. Usually the rickshaws were only big enough to hold one adult person, sometimes with a small child sitting on the adult's lap. I remember that once when I was little I had to sit on the lap of someone I didn't know well, which I did not like at all. I also remember the first time I saw an automobile, a small car belonging to one of the missionaries who lived in the Baptist Compound.

It attracted quite a lot of attention and curiosity, and it was quite a thrill when I and some other children were allowed to take turns standing on the car's running board and holding onto its door for a few minutes!

Some distance outside of the city and located in a big park was King Yu's Terrace. Yu was the ancient emperor who was said to have devised a method to control the Yellow River from flooding. When I was in grade school, the whole school would go there on holidays to have picnics, play games, perform skits, and sing. I remember we always had steamed bread and tea eggs—eggs that were boiled in salt, spices, and tea leaves. We children had great fun! Today, the terrace is a major tourist attraction.

King Yu's Terrace is named after the first emperor of the ancient Xia dynasty, but was built just outside of Kaifeng about six hundred years ago during the Ming dynasty. It has been the site of musical performances and poetry readings for hundreds of years. Here, students of True Light School are shown on a field trip to the terrace. The tall man standing next to the far-left pillar is my father, who was principal of the school for a time.

Chapter 3
THE SOUTH TREE PAVILION AND GRANDMOTHER'S GOATS

南樹樓和奶奶放羊

Although Kaifeng was my home town, my earliest and fondest childhood memories are of the Baptist Compound where my family lived and my siblings and I went to school. The compound was a vast place, surrounded by gray brick walls with thick, sturdy wooden gates. In addition to homes for the teachers and missionaries, and separate school buildings and dormitories for girls and boys, there was a playground with a basketball court, a swing, and a slide. The girls' dormitory was on the south side of the compound, which bordered an area of farm fields. On the east side of the dormitory there was a long row of low willow trees just inside the wire fence dividing the compound from more fields. The trees were close to each other, their branches sometimes touching. We named the area the South Tree Pavilion, and after classes we would go there to play. I remember that we pretended that the trees were beautiful mansions and would swing on the trees as if we were monkeys.

Our house was very big and of a gray-green color, so we called it the Gray House. It had three levels. On the first floor was a living/dining room and a small room off to the side that became my father's study. There was a small room just inside the front door and to the right that eventually became the bedroom of my paternal grandmother. The kitchen was in the back, up a few steps from the back door, and across from the kitchen was a pantry. On the second floor were our bedrooms, and on the third floor was the attic, which was used for storage.

The house had two porches in the front: one on the second floor, enclosed by big windows, and one on the first floor, three steps up from the ground. This porch was surrounded on two sides by wide, cement balustrades. I often sat on one and read books. Growing up, I would read anything I could get my hands on. I read several famous Chinese classics, like *The Dream of the Red Chamber*, written in the Song dynasty, and *Journey to the*

Opposite foreground: Here I am (second from left) as a toddler in 1932 in the Baptist Compound.

Opposite background: Kaifeng was once enclosed by a wall with watchtowers and gates such as this one. The Baptist Compound where my family lived was also surrounded by walls.

West, from the Ming dynasty. I remember reading books that had been translated into Chinese, like *Jane Eyre, Little Women, Heidi,* and *The Twins of Norway.* I read several others, the titles of which I have forgotten, by Russian authors. Frequently, during summer vacation, I would take a book and climb up into a tree near our house to sit on the branches and read. I wanted to avoid the noise of the house and get away from my younger brothers.

Here I am, as a little girl, on the grounds of the Baptist Compound where I grew up.

One hot summer afternoon when I was reading on our lower-level porch, I got tired and decided to lie down on one of the cement balustrades, where I fell asleep. Fortunately, I didn't fall off. On another summer afternoon, when I was about eight years old, I was taking a nap and my bed began to shake. I ran outside and saw people standing in the yard. It was an earthquake, the only one that took place while I lived in Kaifeng. It lasted for only a moment, but I remember it well.

We had a big yard enclosed by a wire fence on two sides and high walls on the other two. Beyond the north wall were streets and neighboring houses; beyond the west wall were farm fields. Inside the yard, at the northwest corner, were several smaller buildings, including an outhouse. Near our house was a deep well used by several families. The well was surrounded by a low brick wall, built to prevent children from falling in. When I was old enough, I often helped to draw water from the well with a bucket and carry it inside the back door of our house, where there stood a huge, deep vat that held many gallons. Half of a hollowed-out gourd always floated on top to scoop out water. We used the water for everything. For bathing, it had to be warmed. For drinking, it had to be boiled.

Between our house and the north wall was a large area where my grandmother planted fruits and vegetables, including watermelons. Kaifeng was known for its watermelons, which grew well because of the sandy soil abundant in northern Henan Province. Because we did not have a refrigerator, we kept the watermelon cold by putting it inside a basket that was suspended from a rope and lowered into the cold water of the well.

We were not rich, but neither were we poor. God supplied all that we needed. Because both my parents taught school, and because labor was very cheap, we hired a cook and a seamstress. Usually such workers were destitute, and happy to find jobs as domestics in homes where food and lodging were provided. In our house, both our cook and seamstress were treated almost as members of the family. Our cook and his family lived in a small house behind ours. Our seamstress, a widow named Wu Haimin—who did not have children of her own—lived in our house, in a small room near the pantry. At that time, one couldn't buy ready-made clothing, so Haimin made all our clothes. She also made our shoes. Haimin didn't have much education, but what a great storyteller she was! Many evenings when we finished our homework we

begged her to tell us stories. We would sit around her as she sewed, listening to her stories—some historically true and some based on ancient legends. We were transfixed by her vivid descriptions! I remember that one day Haimin disappeared and we were all very worried. My grandmother took me to search for her, and we found her in a cemetery at her husband's grave, weeping.

I was very close to my grandmother. My parents had bought a small plot of land with a three-room house in a village two or three miles from the Baptist Compound. There, in that small house, my grandmother lived, raising goats so she could give her grandchildren goat milk to drink. My grandmother hired a middle-aged woman to stay with her and help with cooking and tending the goats. Often, they would walk to our house, carrying small buckets of goat milk. Sometimes during summer vacation I would stay with my grandmother and help her feed and milk the goats. I also remember that in her front yard there were two date trees. When the dates were ripe, I would use a long wooden stick with a forked end to reach up and shake the branches so the dates would drop down. The fresh dates were very tasty. One could also buy dried, pitted dates at the market.

My mother (far right) taught kindergarten in the Girls' School in the Baptist Compound. Here she is holding a violin, with me standing to her right, during an outdoor music class that included some students from the Boys' School.

I loved staying at Grandmother's house. I felt happy and carefree away from my father, who was very strict with me. One time while I was playing with my younger brother Samuel, I accidentally hit him. Although Samuel and I would later become very close, at the time he got angry at me, and ran to the house to tell Father what I had done. I got a spanking. In China, the firstborn son was treasured and held in such high regard that it seemed as if I had done something really wrong!

My grandmother, however, spoiled me, nearly always giving in whenever I asked to have or do something. She took care of washing my hair, which was very thick. I think I was about eight years old when I decided to grow my hair long and wear it braided. It was not easy for my grandmother to wash my hair. We didn't have any shampoo, so she had to use soap bars. She wanted to have my hair cut shorter and thinned out a little, but I refused. Eventually, she had had enough! One afternoon I was taking a nap and I must have been sound asleep. When I awoke, I found that my hair had been cut very short. I had a big tantrum!

About six months after this photo was taken of me and my sister, Lois (right), our brother Samuel—the oldest of our four brothers— would be born.

Chapter 4
SCHOOL DAYS AND SILKWORMS

Miss Zemma Hare lived in a little house not far from the Girls' School and within walking distance of our home. She was beloved by my siblings and me, and we called her Auntie. She told us that America was on the other side of the earth, and if we could dig straight down far enough, we would reach it. She also said that because she came from Orange, Texas, whenever we ate an orange we should think of her.

Auntie had a Chinese cook who learned how to prepare American meals, and it was at her home that I first tasted American food. I remember being in her house quite a few times. While the adults visited, she let Lois and me go into her walk-in closet to look at her things. We saw her Western clothes and shoes and marveled at them. She had a big Sears, Roebuck catalog and we would sit on the floor turning the pages, looking at the strange things in America. More than once she invited us to stay overnight.

From the time I was very young, Auntie had been telling me that when I graduated from high school she would take

me to America to attend college at her alma mater, Mary Hardin-Baylor College, in Belton, Texas. Unfortunately, she got very sick and had to go back to the states to seek treatment. It was the year 1940, before I turned eleven. We went with her to the train station. It was a very sad and tearful farewell knowing we might never see her again, which turned out to be true. Later, when the news came that she had passed away, my mother cried very hard! I did, however, fulfill her hope for me, and attended her alma mater years later.

I think it was because of Auntie's influence that I liked school and was a good student. I started kindergarten at the Girls' School in the Baptist Compound and attended classes there up through the middle of seventh grade. We went to school five-and-a-half days a week, as was the Chinese custom at that time. Every day at midmorning, we attended chapel services. I remember that I was in fifth grade when, at an evangelistic meeting in the school auditorium, I realized that although I had been born in a Christian home, I still needed God's forgiveness to

小學和養蠶

Opposite top: Miss Zemma Hare, a Baptist missionary, was a close friend of my mother's, and one of the most influential people in my life.

Opposite bottom: One of my favorite hobbies when I was growing up was raising silkworms. Here a winged silkworm emerges from its cocoon.

19

find salvation. That was when I accepted Jesus as my personal Savior.

The principal of the Girls' School at that time was Miss Josephine Ward from the United States. In sixth grade, I began to learn English, which was taught by Miss Ward. I had already been exposed to English from spending so much time with Auntie Zemma, and had learned some simple English phrases. But in school we had to learn basic English grammar, including verb tenses and parts of speech. Before long, I could read and write simple English sentences. I remember very clearly one time during our English class we had to compose a short sentence. When we turned in our papers, Miss Ward read them all and then showed my paper in front of the class. She praised me for my neat writing, which made me happy, but also embarrassed.

Miss Ward lived by herself in a little house with a yard inside the Baptist Compound. Sometimes she would invite her pupils to visit. I loved spending time there. Her furniture and the arrangement of the interior of her house intrigued me. Sometimes she would give us American cookies. We all loved her.

The twin sons (second and fourth from left) of an American missionary couple were the first Caucasian children I ever saw.

The first time I saw Caucasian children was during my grade school years, when I was nine or ten years old. They were identical twin boys, sons of an American missionary couple, Rev. and Mrs. Gillespie. We called Rev. Gillespie Ge Mushi (葛牧師), which was meant to resemble the pronunciation of his name, at least to the Chinese ear. Mushi literally means "shepherd teacher" and is used to address pastors. The boys were about the same age as my sister, Lois, but I never saw them in our school and presumed that they were homeschooled. As a result, we didn't interact with them at all. But we saw them in church and thought they were very cute.

Every summer, I attended Bible camps in the compound with my family. The camps lasted about two months. By the time I was eleven years old, I was a devout Christian and knew many of the American missionaries living in the compound, including a young married couple without children. One day the wife got very sick and died. The whole school was in mourning. At her funeral service, we were told not to go to her gravesite, a plot of land at the southwest corner of our schoolyard, where there would be a private family gathering. But some of us were so curious to see everything that we went anyway, very stealthily. We

were found out later and publicly reprimanded! I suffered double jeopardy when I received a severe lecture from my father when he discovered what I had done. But by then, I was too old to be spanked!

In school, I met girls who came from the local villages. They usually had long hair and wore very pretty, dangling earrings. I wanted to be like them. I asked my mother to have my earlobes pierced so I could also wear such earrings. My mother said no, and explained that because we were Christians we didn't believe in Chinese superstitions. According to one such superstition, the devil would snatch anything perfect, and when the ears were pierced the body became imperfect and the devil would not touch it. For this reason, most small Chinese boys had one earlobe pierced and wore one earring. However, I was quite satisfied with my mother's explanation and never asked again.

My best childhood friend was Gao Yurui (高育睿), who was about two years older than I. We lived next door to each other and both went to the Girls' School in the compound, where her mother was also a teacher. We always walked to school and played together. Yurui had one younger brother, Yumin (高育民). I never met her father, and many years later Yurui

Top: My best childhood friend was Gao Yurui, here on the right with me in the Baptist Compound in 1933.

Bottom: I was sad to lose touch with Yurui (right) as we grew older, but we would reunite as adults in 1979.

In our free time, my siblings and I found lots of ways to have fun. Although we were not poor, we had no money to buy anything luxurious, such as a bicycle, and we made most of our own toys. I remember building kites by splitting bamboo branches into thin strips and polishing them until smooth. Then I soaked them in boiling water to make them soft and pliable. I bent each strip and tied the ends together in the shape of either a bird or a butterfly, and glued rice paper around the frame. I cut more paper into narrow strips to make a tail, and attached a long string to the center of the kite. We also made kaleidoscopes out of three strips of clear glass shaped into a triangle, with small pieces of colored glass or broken pottery sealed into the bottom section of the triangle on top of another piece of glass.

When Lois and I were very young, we were each given a doll by a missionary returning from furlough in America. They were the only dolls we ever received, and they were greatly treasured. However, I don't really remember playing with mine much because I preferred playing more active games, including marbles. When I was older I learned to knit. I made my own knitting needles of different sizes by splitting bamboo branches and polishing

told me he had left them when she was very young. So there were just the three of them in their family. After my family moved out of the Baptist Compound, Yurui and I lost contact with each other. I knew she had married and had become a teacher in Xi'an, about three hundred miles west of Kaifeng. But I would not learn what happened to her family for almost forty years.

them until smooth. Another hobby was raising silkworms for amusement. It was very interesting to watch a silkworm go through metamorphosis, transforming from its tiny, black, thread-like stage into an actual worm about one to one and a half inches in length and about one quarter of an inch in circumference. When the silkworm was in its very first stage, I would put it inside an empty matchbox lined with a thin piece of cotton and put the box inside my pocket for warmth to speed up the worm's growth. When the worm was big enough to be taken out of the box, I put it on a small piece of cloth and fed it mulberry leaves, its favorite food, which my friends and I would pick from mulberry trees in the nearby forests. When the worm was ready to spin silk, it would stop eating and its head would become enlarged and raised. It was looking for something on which to spin its silk! I would get a small tree branch and put the worm on the branch, where it would spew a silk cocoon in which it enclosed itself. After a while it would chew an opening in the cocoon and emerge as an insect with wings, which would then lay eggs. At least, this is the way I remember it.

Chapter 5

PEARL HARBOR DAY

Looking back, I realize that I grew up in tumultuous times. In 1937, Japan—having already conquered Korea—invaded China through Manchuria, beginning the Sino-Japanese War. In one major battle, Japanese troops attacked the Lugouqiao (Marco Polo) Bridge located about nine miles southwest of Beijing. The bridge was famous for the hundreds of stone lions lining both its sides. I learned to sing a very old ballad about the bridge as a young child. The Japanese bombing missions began encroaching farther and farther into mainland China, reaching Kaifeng the following year. To avoid some of the danger, Auntie Zemma took my mother, me, Lois, and Samuel, who was only two years old, on the train to a retreat house at the top of Rooster Mountain in the southern part of Henan Province. The retreat house was where the Baptist missionaries spent their summer vacations. However, it was winter and very cold, especially on the mountaintop, and we moved into a small, unheated, three-bedroom house farther down the mountainside in a more protected,

wooded area. We all crowded inside the little house, with Auntie Zemma taking up one room. I remember that one morning, as I walked along the narrow path to the outhouse, I met a mountain goat. He was big and had long, curved horns, and he frightened me. When I tried to get by, he refused to move, so I retreated. While we lived on the mountain, our mother helped us keep up with our schoolwork. Auntie Zemma gave us English lessons and taught us to sing "A Shelter in the Time of Storm," a hymn that came to mean a great deal in my life.

We returned to Kaifeng after about two months, even though Japanese airplanes were still dropping bombs. There, one of the buildings in the Baptist Compound had a flat roof. Painted on the roof was a giant American flag, a signal to the bombers that the building was American property. Still, we often took part in drills to be ready for a possible attack, going into the basement of the school for some measure of safety. I remember one time during an air raid when a bomb did hit the roof of the school building. Thanks to

偷襲珍珠港

Opposite foreground: In this family photo dated December 10, 1940, I am standing in the back, on the right, next to Lois. My mother is holding Joseph and my father is holding Eugene. Samuel is seated in the middle of the front row.

Opposite background: A mountain goat terrified me on Rooster Mountain in 1937 when I was seven years old.

Here I am (right) with Lois (middle) and one of our cousins in a grade school photo taken in a photography studio.

the public-address system telling all students to go downstairs to the main floor and gather in the school auditorium. We were given no idea of what had happened. Those of us who lived with our parents within the compound were told to immediately go home, and the students who lived in the dormitories were told to get in touch with their families and tell them to come pick them up.

I gathered my books and walked home, a distance of about one mile. Already lining the road where I had to walk were Japanese soldiers on horseback with swords attached to the ends of their guns. Although the Japanese had been occupying Kaifeng since 1939, I had never before seen soldiers in the compound, and had felt safe. That is because it was American property. But now that Japan was also at war with America, I was really frightened.

When I got home, I found my mother and grandmother frantically packing suitcases and bags and whatever else they could find to fill with our belongings. I was told that now that the United States had entered the war, the Japanese were taking over the compound and that we had to get out by six o'clock that afternoon. In the meantime, the American missionaries who had been working at the compound were taken by Japanese soldiers to an

a miracle from God it did not explode. It bounced off the corner of the building and landed nearby, where it destroyed several trees. One day about that same time, my father was sitting at his desk at home, in a small office next to our dining area. The desk was set up against a wooden side door not used as an entrance. Suddenly a bullet penetrated the door, slightly grazing my father's head and landing in the wall behind him. We never did find out where the bullet came from.

In America, Pearl Harbor Day was December 7, 1941. But in China, it was already the morning of December 8. I remember it was a Monday and I was in an English class in seventh grade. Suddenly we heard an announcement on internment camp where they were held until they were able to secure passage to the United States. I never saw any of them again! It was one of the saddest and most traumatic days of my life. By then, Joseph had been born and I remember wondering, where could such a large family go on such short notice? Thank God for my grandmother's little house not far away, where we could stay temporarily until we could move into Kaifeng.

By this time, my father had become a pastor in the Baptist Church. In 1935, when I was almost five years old, he had traveled to the United States, where he lived for three years, studying first at Southwestern Baptist Theological Seminary in Fort Worth, Texas, before transferring to Southern Baptist Theological Seminary in Louisville, Kentucky. In 1937, he received a master's degree in theology from Southern Baptist. When my father returned to China, I was seven years old. I remember thinking he looked very distinguished in his Western suit. Almost immediately after arriving in Kaifeng, he was ordained a Baptist minister and became pastor at the Gulou Street Baptist Church, the first Baptist Church in Kaifeng. He had also joined the faculty of the new Baptist seminary

established in Kaifeng in 1938. There he taught introductory Greek, religious education, evangelism, and theology. He was the only Chinese member of the faculty. He also continued to teach at the Boys' School in the Baptist Compound.

Due to the foresight of some elders in the Chinese Baptist Church, including my father—who had sensed the anti-American sentiment of the Japanese government—the church had raised money to purchase a large plot of land in the center of Kaifeng the year before the bombing of Pearl Harbor. On the property, which had both inner and outer courtyards, there were several houses and a well. The area was enclosed by a wall and a gate that could be locked at night for security. The street entering this area was named Fried Rice Lane. Because my parents had helped pay for the land, which had room for about three families, they were granted one of the houses on the property. The elders of the church decided to take down the wall between two other houses built back-to-back to make a larger room for church services. Wooden benches without backs were bought and used as pews. Sunday worship services continued there much as they had at the Baptist Compound.

Foreground: My cousin Cheng Xiufang, the youngest daughter of my mother's oldest sister, is ten years older than I. Still, we were very close and have kept in touch all our lives.

Background: Kaifeng was the capital city of China during the Northern Song dynasty. The buildings that once served as headquarters for the government, such as this one, are known as the Kaifeng Fu and now house museums.

Chapter 6

THE LITTLE RED COMPOUND AND LIFE UNDER OCCUPATION

Following the attack on Pearl Harbor, our schooling was completely disrupted. My parents sent Lois and me to live and go to school in the Little Red Compound south of the city. The word *Red* in its name was due to the red-colored tiles on the roofs of all the buildings in the compound. In its outer courtyard was one building with two levels that was located close to the street and used for a church, and another building toward the back that was used as a school. In the inner courtyard there were houses for faculty members and other families.

In the Little Red Compound, Lois and I lived with one of the teachers, a dear friend of my mother's we called Auntie Wong. We shared the second, small bedroom in her house with another student, a girl about eight years older than I whom Auntie Wong had befriended and taken in. Our room was very crowded, but because we didn't have many things, we didn't need much space. Still, I wasn't very happy there. I missed my family, and even though I didn't know how to cook, I had to help Auntie Wong prepare our meals.

During this time, with the area still occupied by the Japanese, the Chinese Nationalist government began bombing Japanese military bases. I remember the sirens periodically blasting warnings to the public, alerting everyone to seek shelter. There were trenches dug along a wall behind our school in the Little Red Compound. The alarm sounded one day at noontime when we were eating lunch in the classroom and we had to leave everything and run to the shelter. There was no cloud cover overhead and we could see bombs falling from the sky. If they had been directly over us, we would have died because, as it turned out, the shelter was only for avoiding injuries from flying shrapnel. Once the bombing was over, we went back to the classroom and found our bowls of noodles covered with dust that had dropped from the ceiling!

Meanwhile, in Kaifeng, the Japanese occupation was putting a strain on my family. My father was arrested one day and accused of cooperating with the American government. He was beaten and put

小紅樓和日軍佔領下的生活

in confinement. Some good people of the church came forward to testify that he was a teacher and pastor of a Chinese church, and had nothing to do with the American government. He was freed, but still it was truly a frightening experience!

Some of the Japanese soldiers were very cruel. The well-known Rape of Nanking and other atrocities they had committed have been well recorded in history. Before the Japanese took over our city we had learned in geography class that the map of China was like a mulberry leaf and Japan was like a silkworm. The same way the silkworm slowly ate up a mulberry leaf, Japan gradually encroached on Chinese territory. The Japanese occupation of Kaifeng reminded me of this lesson.

However, it was not only Japanese soldiers who had come to Kaifeng, but also civilian Japanese families who were Christian and who established their own churches. My father got to know one of the Japanese pastors and invited him to speak in our church and eat dinner with us. It did not bother us that he was Japanese. It was interesting to meet him, and we accepted him as a fellow Christian and held no animosity toward him and his family.

After a few months at the Little Red Compound, Lois and I rejoined our family, transferring to yet another school. This one my father had set up in the far western part of Kaifeng. That was where we completed the school year. The school had only two teachers—my father was one of them—and only two other pupils. What I remember most about the rest of that year is that each of the students received a lot of attention!

The following year, Lois and I entered a Catholic girls' junior high school in the northeastern corner of the city. I was in eighth grade, and Lois was in sixth. We went to school there for one year. To get to this school, we had to walk a few miles, which took more than an hour each way. I wore out several pairs of cloth shoes! Because my feet were growing too fast for new shoes to be made for me, I often had to wear shoes with holes in them. I was very embarrassed. But it was better than what my mother and grandmothers had endured: having their feet bound.

Our mother would give my sister and me each a steamed bun and a few coins every morning. We used the money to buy some roasted beef from the families of Jewish descent—the Kaifeng Jews—who lived along our way to school. I remember they looked just like other Chinese because of hundreds of years of intermarriage. They did not eat pork but the roast beef they sold was delicious. Every day when we passed their street we would each buy a piece of roast beef and put it in our buns to have as lunch. We were allowed to eat lunch in the school library, where I would browse the library for books of interest. We were permitted to read the books, but not to take them out. One of the books I remember reading there was *Alice in Wonderland* translated into Chinese.

Sometimes on our way to and from school, Lois and I would stop to see my mother's oldest sister and her daughters, our cousins Cheng Xiufang (程秀芳) and Cheng Xiulian (程秀蓮). Her oldest daughter, Cheng Xiuzheng (程秀貞), was already married and living with her husband. I remember that my aunt, who by then was widowed, always gave us something to eat. Lois and I became especially close to Xiufang, even though she was ten years older than I. My parents had helped her and Xiulian with their education, arranging for them to attend the Girls' School in the Baptist Compound, and live in the girls' dormitory there. Frequently, my parents would invite them to eat with us. Years later when I traveled back to China, I visited Xiufang and Xiuzheng and their families, and the family of Xiulian, who died in her forties after raising four children.

After one year at the Catholic school, Lois and I transferred to True Light School, where I finished ninth and tenth grades. That school, in the center of Kaifeng near the ancient Drum Tower, was operated by the Chinese Baptists. I remember that I was in charge of walking through the halls ringing a handbell to mark the end of each class period.

It was in August 1945, during the summer after tenth grade, that Japan surrendered to the Allied forces, ending World War II and the Japanese occupation of China. I remember that we were very happy. Some of the civilian Japanese families living in Kaifeng that we had gotten to know moved back to Japan. But some of the Japanese soldiers who had treated our people cruelly were rounded up by Chinese officials and put to work repairing the railroads they had destroyed. I saw them working on the railroad with my own eyes. They were very humiliated, but not ill-treated. Once the war ended, the Baptist Compound was restored to the church, and my family returned there to live.

However, even after the Japanese surrendered, China didn't have much time to enjoy peace. The Communist army was advancing from western China toward the east, and in the summer of 1946, while my family was attending a Bible camp, soldiers came very near Kaifeng. At night, we could hear the sound of cannons and gunfire, and I remember often going to bed fully dressed in case we had to make a fast escape.

I began keeping a journal, made from rice paper, when I was in junior high school. This page is from the summer of 1946 when I was fifteen years old, and tells about hearing gunfire at night. We thought it was the Communist army getting close to our hometown. Later we learned that the incident was actually related to a family feud in the area.

十三日　星期二　　晴

昨夜炮声把我们從夢中驚醒了，我还没有從床上起來，香娥慌々忙々的走到我屋裡說：「趕快起來吧！八路攻進來了。」我听了，如同青天響了一声霹靂，我想不过是放儿声炮陣庄陣庄周圍罷了，八路軍怎能攻得這樣快呢，我疑信参々半的披衣起床了。

輕々的走到她们屋裏只見她们都已起來，有的在窗口此望，有的跪在床沿禱告，芬瑞見我去，悄声和我說道：「姐姐，你看樓门前，大槐樹下坐的那一堆人。」他们是從外面逃進來的，我向外一望，果見有一堆人，还隱約的听見場々私語的聲音，文鳳姐說：「不要再看了，咱跪下禱吉吧。」我们就都跪下誠心的祈求神的保佑，以後沒有甚麼動静，又睡了一会兒，天才明了。

起來洗了臉，我们下樓去问々晚上到底是怎麼一回事，後來听說並不是八路軍，是北院住的人，扔了兩個手榴弹，並有個人被炸死了，还有一個受了重

Chapter 7

HIGH SCHOOL, RICE PAPER JOURNALS, AND ROBBERS IN THE NIGHT

In the fall of 1945, just after the Japanese surrender, I changed schools again, moving to Sacred Virtue School, a Christian secondary school in Zhengzhou, about two hours from Kaifeng by train. The school had been founded by its principal, Wu Huimin (吴惠民), whose name means "benefit or kindness to people." Formerly a high-ranking officer in the Chinese Nationalist army under General Chiang Kai-shek, he had converted to Christianity and started a school for poor students whose families could not afford expensive public schools. In the 1940s, to avoid the advancing Communist troops during the Chinese Civil War, Principal Wu moved the entire student body, faculty, and the faculty members' families—a group of more than eight hundred people—from Zhengzhou west to a location near Xi'an. Their journey, which took longer than two months, was mostly made on foot, but whenever possible oxcarts or other vehicles were used to carry the children and the sick. The group eventually found a large compound owned by a wealthy family who had moved away, leaving a manager in charge. Principal Wu successfully negotiated with him to use the site as a short-term location for the school.

Sacred Virtue moved back to the Zhengzhou area in the summer of 1944 and reopened just outside the city in a park that served as a burial ground for Chinese soldiers. It was a very picturesque place with many trees and small mounds here and there, some of which had beautiful pavilions built on top. This is where I was sent for my last two years of high school. Although I was only fourteen years old, my father wanted me to attend Sacred Virtue because of its reputation for being academically excellent and spiritually sound. It was the first time I was away from home for an extended period of time. I remember my father taking me to school on the train, and the many times I was so homesick that I cried myself to sleep. I got to know other girls

高中，米紙上的日記，和夜間不速之客

A studio photograph of me (back row, right) with some of my Sacred Virtue classmates. One is Du Anluo (front row, left), whom we called Hannah. She was older than I and took me under her wing. Also in the photo is a married friend of ours (front row, middle) wearing her hair pulled back in a bun, the custom for married women at the time.

who stayed in the same dormitory, which actually was a building that had housed soldiers. It had no furniture or beds, but only low, cement platforms on which we slept. Looking back, life was rough for me and my young classmates.

When I got to be good friends with a few of the girls, I started to feel better and less homesick. One girl, Du Anluo (杜安樂), whom we called Hannah, was about four years older than I and acted as my big sister, taking me under her wing, so to speak. Little did I know that our paths would cross

several times later in our lives. I made two other lifelong friends at Sacred Virtue: my deskmate, Chen Heping (陳和平), whom we called Esther and who lives in Brea, California; and Xie Deling (謝德玲), who lives in San Francisco.

Principal Wu was not physically strong due to heart trouble. He had to leave our school and move to a countryside villa to rest and recover. The eldest of his daughters and I had become good friends and stayed in touch for many years. One Sunday afternoon she and another friend and I decided to visit him. It was too far to walk, so we hired three donkeys to take us there. It was quite an experience! Thinking about it reminds me of the photograph I have of my mother riding on a donkey on her way to my father's village after their wedding!

The school had no place for a kitchen. Food was prepared in an iron wok set in a brick fire pit. Firewood was used as fuel. The school hired a cook to make our meals. We paid for groceries, and I was put in charge of the funds because I was the only one with a small suitcase that could be locked. I remember that I was very reluctant to eat the food because many times I could see tiny worms floating in the pot. However, I became hungry and had to force myself to eat it.

Behind our dormitory building was a low, mud brick wall. One night while we slept, a thief jumped the wall, came into our dormitory, and stole everything we had, including my suitcase with our grocery money inside. The other dormitories had not been disturbed, but when we woke up, we found that even the clothing we had left at our bedsides was gone. I now owned only the pajamas I had slept in and had to borrow something to wear from a friend living in another dormitory until I could get word to my parents to send me some clothes. After this incident, the school stationed a few male students outside the low wall to stand guard. However, I don't know how they could have helped us if a thief decided to come and steal again!

After some time at Sacred Virtue, I suspected I was not well. I felt very warm, especially in the afternoons, and was unusually tired. Looking back, I realize I was probably running a low-grade fever. Unbeknownst to me, I had two good friends at school who had contracted tuberculosis but did not know it. Because we all dipped our chopsticks into the same pot or bowl to get our food, this would soon prove to be a serious problem for me as well.

On Sundays, my friends and I walked several miles into Zhengzhou for worship services. There we would part to attend our own denominational churches. I would go to the Baptist church and they to either the Lutheran or Methodist church. We would find each other afterward and walk back to school together. One day on our way back from church we saw the body of a man hanging on a tree. It was a frightening sight. Later, we found out that he was a robber who had been caught and hung. His body had been left on the public road as a warning to others.

It was during junior high school that I began keeping a journal, which I continued—off and on—for some years. It began as a requirement in my Chinese language, literature, and composition class. I remember that my friends and I actually began writing in two separate journals: one for our teacher, and another one—that included things we didn't want the teacher to know—for ourselves. In the Chinese culture, we generally don't express our feelings very freely, and my journal became a good way for me to write about how I felt about school, and, later, my life. Up until August 1951, I wrote in Chinese. Later, I wrote in English. I made the journals out of rice paper and sewed the pages together with embroidery thread. I also made my own ink using a solid black ink stick made of

聖高首屆畢業同學留影

There were only six girls in my class when I graduated from high school, and three of the others were sisters. I am fourth from the left in the front row.

vegetable soot and glue. I had to grind the ink with water on a special ink stone to produce liquid ink. I wrote with a bamboo brush with a very fine tip made from animal hair.

Every year on March 8, which was designated as Women's Day, we were encouraged to write essays or poems. Our papers were pasted on a large, wooden board mounted on a wall for others to read. Both boys and girls were encouraged to contribute. My senior year, I wrote a poem and titled it "Brave Sisters, Unite!" in praise of women in general. I still have the original copy.

I graduated from high school in 1947 at the age of sixteen, and in the first class to graduate from Sacred Virtue after the school moved back to Zhengzhou. I was the youngest in my class, which included twenty-three boys but only six girls. (Three of the girls were sisters, and the youngest was my friend Esther.) That's because at the time it was still uncommon for girls to go to high school. Unfortunately, it was a tumultuous time of fighting between the Chinese Nationalist and Communist regimes, and there was no graduation ceremony for my class. We didn't even get diplomas. Later on, when

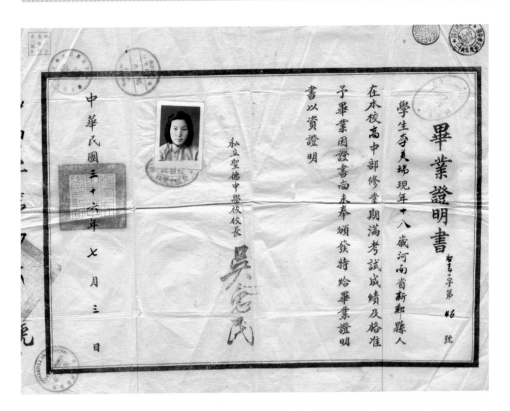

畢業證明書

學生李美瑞現年十八歲河南省新鄭縣人

在本校高中部修業期滿考試成績及格准

予畢業因證書尚未奉頒發特給畢業證明

書以資證明

私立聖德中學校校長 吳宮民

中華民國三十六年 七 月 三 日

that was made known to the school, I was issued a certificate with some official seals on it to prove that I did indeed graduate from high school. The only diploma I have ever received was the one given to me when I graduated from college in the United States.

At the end of the school year, my father and sister came to bring me home. We had to ride a coal-powered train for many miles, passing through mountain tunnels and over bridges. The train was so crowded that even with tickets we had very little room, and we were forced to sit on top of the train, which fortunately had side rails to hold on to. When we passed inside the tunnels we had to bend down in order not to have our heads lopped off, and hold our breath to avoid inhaling too much smoke. Each time, it lasted many minutes, and was miserable. We emerged from the train with blackened faces and clothing! We were very happy to get home, take a good bath, and change clothes.

Because of political upheaval at the time, I never received an official high school diploma. This graduation certificate confirms that I completed high school satisfactorily.

37

438183　No. 京字10815

特　身　籍　職　年　姓
徵　量　貫　業　歲　名
　　　河　教　十　李
　　　南　　　八　美
　　　士　　　歲　瑞

Chapter 8
TUBERCULOSIS AND TURBULENT TIMES

I had always planned that after I graduated from high school I would go with my father to the United States, where he would pursue his doctorate in theology from Southern Baptist Theological Seminary and I would enter Mary Hardin-Baylor College.

The summer after I finished high school, my father and I took the train to Shanghai to apply for passports from the Chinese Nationalist government and visas from the American Consulate. To get the visas, my father and I each had to undergo a thorough physical examination. We got our passports, but my physical examination revealed that I had spots on my lungs caused by tuberculosis, and I was refused passage to America. Of course, I now realize that I most likely had contracted it from my classmates at Sacred Virtue. At that time, active TB was not treated and was usually fatal. Several years later, I found out that my friends died from the disease. I was fortunate to have escaped that fate. I was shocked and deeply disappointed, as were my parents. My father and I returned to Kaifeng, and that September he sailed alone to the States, where he would study for the next three years.

My physical examination also revealed that my eyesight was quite poor. Actually, I had suspected for many years that I needed glasses. Although I always asked to be seated in the front of the classroom, I struggled to see notes written on the blackboard. However, I was still able to pass all my exams. I never told my parents because I really didn't want to wear glasses. I had seen other people wearing glasses and thought they were ugly. Maybe I was conceited. When I finally did get glasses, after my physical in Shanghai, I could see details that before had been just a blur. And the glasses were better looking than I had thought they would be.

Meanwhile, in addition to having been accepted at Mary Hardin-Baylor College, I had taken two college entrance examinations—one for the University of Nanking and one for the Medical Institute at the University of Shanghai—and was very happy about passing both of them.

肺病和動蕩的日子

Opposite: I received my first passport in 1947.

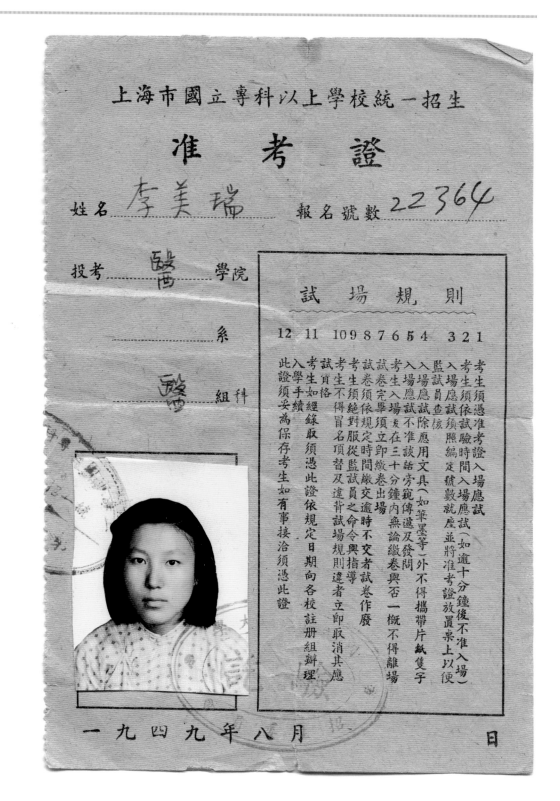

However, due to my illness, I could attend neither. Although I did not feel sick, I was running a low-grade fever and felt tired most afternoons. I also felt helpless and useless, and fell into a deep depression, certain that I was a great burden to my mother.

At the time my father left for the United States, he believed we would be safe in Kaifeng. No one knew how powerful the Communists had become or that they would try to get control of all of China. But by December 1947, my father realized he had been wrong. The Communist army had pushed again to the outskirts of Kaifeng and he cabled my mother, telling her to leave the city and go south, perhaps to Shanghai. He wanted the entire family to make plans to join him in the United States as soon as possible. He had no way of knowing it would be almost five and a half years before our family would be together again.

At first, my mother could do nothing but pray and seek God's guidance. How could she, a woman who had never traveled far, get herself, her six children, and my aged grandmother—who was living with us—out of the city, let alone to America? But my mother was resourceful. When she heard that the China Inland Mission Hospital in Kaifeng was planning to evacuate all the American doctors and nurses by chartered airplanes, she met with a hospital official, telling him I was sick and asking if I could travel with them to Shanghai, the first stop in a journey that she hoped would take me to America. The official agreed, but told her no one knew exactly what day the Americans would be able to leave, and because we had no telephone, they could not notify her of the date. In the end, someone suggested that I enter the hospital, wait there, and notify my mother once the date was set.

Fortunately, I had a good friend, a student nurse named Li Ruilan (李瑞蘭), who lived in one of the rooms in the hospital. She very graciously allowed me to stay with her. I packed a small suitcase with clothing and a little bag with a few other things I might need. I was anxious about leaving my home alone and not knowing if I would ever see my family again!

Finally, one day in the early spring of 1948, I flew out of Kaifeng to Shanghai in a chartered plane with the American doctors and nurses. My sister and brother Samuel were able to fly out on the next flight. That was a miracle, because officially there was no room on the plane for two more people, even two very small people

Opposite: This was the permit I needed to take the entrance examination for the Medical Institute at the University of Shanghai, which I passed.

This 1947 family photo was taken just before my father left for the United States. Back row, left to right: Me, James, Joseph, Eugene, and Lois. Front row, left to right: Samuel, my mother, my grandmother Nai-Nai, and my father.

who didn't weigh much and wouldn't take up much space. However, a missionary booked on the flight had a big trunk he was planning to take with him. At the last minute, he decided to leave it behind. The combined weight of my sister and brother equaled the weight of the trunk, so they were both allowed on the plane.

I was so happy to see them when they arrived in Shanghai! My father had arranged for me to stay with a friend of his, a Mr. Wu (鄔清芬), but when Lois and Samuel arrived, he took us to the local Baptist Compound, where we lived for several weeks. Lois and I stayed in a little room that was actually a walk-in closet,

and Samuel was housed by another family living in the compound.

Meanwhile, back in Kaifeng, an acquaintance of my father's came to my mother and said that he was going to Shanghai for business and if she wanted to leave he would help her. But they had to wait until the railroad tracks, sections of which had been destroyed by the Communists, had been repaired. When word came that the first train was leaving Kaifeng, my mother purchased tickets for the trip, despite advice that it might not be safe to travel on the very first train to use the newly repaired railroad tracks. My mother did not care. All she wanted was to get out of Kaifeng.

By then, my grandmother had decided she did not want to leave Kaifeng. She said that she was too old to travel. She told my mother, "You go to see my son, and I will die in China." Like me, she feared she would never see anyone in her family again. Although she had two other daughters, they were married and lived elsewhere, and she had never lived with either one of them. However, one of her other granddaughters, along with her own young daughter, came to stay with my grandmother after our family left Kaifeng.

When my mother and my three youngest brothers finally left Kaifeng, in April 1948, they had a frightening experience on the train. It stopped along the way and could not proceed for some reason. Not long after, another train pulled up alongside and was supposed to leave before the train my mother was on. Many people started to climb onto the second train, but my mother wasn't sure what to do. She prayed and read her Bible, seeking guidance from God. She came upon a verse: "Be still and know that I am God." As a result, she did not move. Finally, the train she and my brothers were on started up again; before long it caught up with the second train, which had been stopped and boarded by bandits who had robbed the passengers.

This passport, issued to me in August 1947, expired three years later and before I was actually able to use it.

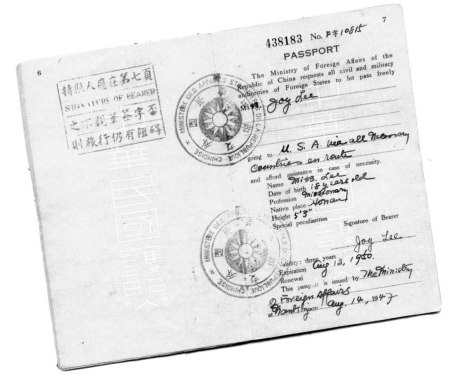

44

Chapter 9
THE FALL OF SHANGHAI

My mother and brothers ended up traveling as far as Suzhou, about an hour west of Shanghai. Known as the Venice of the Orient, Suzhou was a very historic and picturesque city. A month later, Lois, Samuel, and I joined them there, where we rented a small room from a Christian lady who lived in a house on the bank of the Suzhou River, which was actually a canal. A short time after we arrived, we learned from the newspapers that Kaifeng had been taken over by the Communists. I remember feeling thankful for our escape, but also crying out of sadness and fear for our relatives and friends remaining there.

In Suzhou, my five siblings started going to a Christian school. I entered a Christian hospital for rest and treatment. Li Ruilan, the student nurse I had stayed with at the China Inland Mission Hospital in Kaifeng, had somehow made it to Suzhou, too, and was working in this same hospital. I was overjoyed to see her again! Meanwhile, even with my father wiring money from the United States, it soon became too expensive for me to stay in the hospital. After I left, my mother invited Ruilan to our home several times for a meal and to visit with me. But most of the time I had nothing to do to pass the time but read and knit sweaters for my brothers.

On December 9, 1948, we all moved to Shanghai, which was, and still is, the largest city in China. There it was much easier to receive letters and funds from my father. We found a small, narrow house to live in that was connected in a row with other, identical houses. I still remember the address: Peng-Lai Road, Lane #388, Door #4. Our house had a front door and a back door and was built on three levels. The ground floor had a kitchen and a dining area. A small space under the stairway held a commode. The second floor had two small bedrooms, and the third floor, one more bedroom.

I shared the third-floor bedroom with my grandmother. Although she had been reluctant to travel, she missed us so much that she had finally consented to come to Shanghai. Having been so close to her all my life, I had missed her greatly, and

上海的淪陷

Opposite foreground: By early 1949 my grandmother had joined us in Shanghai. Here I am with her (middle) and my mother (right), who was responsible for supporting all of us during some very desperate times.

Opposite background: Shanghai fell to the Communists under Mao Tse-tung in 1949.

45

was very happy when she arrived, accompanied by my cousin, who had lived with her for a time in Kaifeng, and my cousin's daughter. They all stayed with us in our crowded house for a short while before my cousin and her daughter returned to Kaifeng. My grandmother, who at the time was already about eighty years old, seemed quite content. She was not a person to be idle, and kept busy helping with the cooking, washing, and other chores.

By the spring of 1949, many wealthy Chinese had already fled to Hong Kong or Taiwan in advance of the Communist army, fearing persecution, jail, or even death. And my father desperately wanted all of us to get out, too. Due to my illness, I was unable to travel, and Lois was first to go, thanks to yet another miracle. Every day, for several days in a row that May, my mother took public transportation to the airline ticket office downtown to try to buy Lois a ticket to fly from Shanghai to Hong Kong. But repeatedly she was told they were all sold out. Finally, one day the agent said, "I perceive you must be a Christian." My mother told him she was. The agent said, "I am not, but I have a good friend who is. If there should be a cancellation, I will save the ticket for you. So, keep coming back every day." Finally, there was a cancellation, and my mother was able to buy Lois's ticket.

As it turned out, Lois was on what would be the last flight out of Shanghai. Six days later, at about noontime, we saw smoke rising from the shipbuilding factory on the south side of the city not far from the district where we lived. The smoke was so heavy that even the sun was obscured, and the sky was darkened as if night was falling. I remember that the sun, which I could gaze at directly with my naked eye, looked like the moon. At the time, we had no idea what had happened, but the next day we found out that the Chinese Nationalist government leaders had retreated to the island of Taiwan, sailing away in the early morning hours after having set fire to the entire shipbuilding yard.

Without any newspapers available or vendors on the street, news was hard to come by, and the city seemed to come to a standstill. Schools were all shut down and we didn't dare to go anywhere. Overnight the value of the national currency had been drastically reduced. Suddenly, it cost twice as much to buy a dozen eggs. Within a few days, the Communist army arrived. Shanghai had fallen to the Communists, and with it, the whole of China!

After some time, for most of us, order returned and life went on. Meanwhile, in Hong Kong, Lois stayed for nine days in

a little room in the Hillwood Road Baptist Church. Also living at the church was its assistant pastor, who was a former student of my father's, and his family. Lois then flew to Los Angeles, with stops first in Manila, Wake Island, Guam, and Honolulu. She sent a cable to our father to tell him of her arrival. But he did not receive it because he was in Macon, Georgia, attending a summer conference. Lois waited at Los Angeles International Airport, frightened and forlorn! A teacher named Marion Copleston, who had been on the same flight as my sister, noticed her distress and took Lois to her home,

leaving her phone number at the airline office in case our father arrived there later. After two days with no contact from our father, Miss Copleston reported the situation to officials at the Chinese Consulate, who were able to locate him. He sent Lois an airplane ticket to Atlanta, and arranged for a friend attending the conference with him to drive him to the airport to meet her.

Following the conference, my father and Lois took the train to New York City, where they stayed for two months while my father studied at Columbia University and Lois took a sophomore English class

Left: After the fall of Shanghai, order returned to the city. Here my brothers Joseph (left) and Eugene (right) explore the streets of the city in 1949 with the little boy of a family friend.

Right: I found life in Shanghai depressing, although I did have fun playing with a friend and her kitten. And I finally got my glasses. I couldn't believe how much better I could see, and was pleased to discover that they didn't look as bad as I had feared.

at Washington Irving High School. From there they moved to Washington, DC.

With my sister gone, our home seemed empty and I was lonelier than ever. I was depressed that I was not in college and found my life very boring. Looking back, I realize those were desperate days, especially for my mother. The strain of surviving, let alone supporting five children, fell mostly on her shoulders. Her health began to deteriorate, and again, I felt like a burden. My father was still wiring money to support us, and my mother used some of it to pay for me to enter Shanghai's Bethany Lutheran Hospital, where I could have complete bed rest, something I couldn't get at home. But because I really didn't feel sick and wasn't receiving any

treatment, I found it hard to stay in bed all the time. In the hospital, I had a roommate I will only identify by her English name, Eula, who was just one year younger than I. We had known each other in our hometown of Kaifeng, where her father was a teacher and we had been schoolmates—but not really friends—in middle school. Because she was a year behind me, I hadn't known her very well. In the hospital, though, I quickly learned that she was a difficult person to be with and we didn't talk to each other much. She was unkind to the nurses, and when told to lie down, she would not obey, and instead would argue. I remember that she became infatuated with one cute, little nurse, and often turned on the call light, a red light

Here I am (far right) with a group of nurses from Bethany Lutheran Hospital enjoying some fresh air.

above our door. When this nurse answered the call, Eula would make some silly request. Sometimes, I felt embarrassed for her. The only good memory I have of Eula from that time was sneaking outside with her when no one was watching.

Meanwhile, my father had been busy with his studies, and in May 1950, earned his PhD in theology from the Southern Baptist Theological Seminary. However, before long it again became too expensive for him to send enough money back to China to both support our large family and to pay for my stay in the hospital. So, after about three months, and before I was discharged officially, my mother took me home to continue my bed rest.

By the summer of 1949, my sister, Lois, was in Washington, DC.

In May 1950, my father earned his PhD in theology from the Southern Baptist Theological Seminary in Louisville, Kentucky.

Chapter 10
SNEAKING INTO HONG KONG

My parents wanted me to go to the United States for medical treatment, fearing that I would never get well otherwise. But how was I going to travel even as far as Hong Kong? We really had to trust God to work things out, and He did. A Shanghai pastor my mother knew was aware of our predicament. When he found out that a businessman who frequently traveled to Hong Kong was planning to go there with his wife and daughter, he introduced the man to my mother, who asked if I could travel with them. He agreed. It was sometime in July 1950, and after much trouble, that my mother was finally able to get a travel permit for me. I packed a small suitcase with only the bare necessities, which included a few changes of clothing, my Bible, and the diaries that I had kept in my high school years. In another small bag, I carried a few imperishable food items. We had to travel by train for three days to get to Guangzhou, the city on the Chinese mainland closest to Hong Kong, which at the time was under British rule. On the train, we had to sit on hard, wooden benches on either side of a narrow table. It was the most miserable ride imaginable, with the possible exception of the time I rode home on the roof of the train after finishing high school!

We had to spend a night in a Guangzhou hotel, where the couple, their daughter, and I all slept in one double bed! After three days on the train I felt very dirty and fatigued, and slept fully dressed. The next day, I was told that to get into Hong Kong I must cut off my long braids, wear a straw laborer's hat, and take off my eyeglasses so that I would look more like a local farm girl than a student from mainland China. That was because Hong Kong was already overly populated with refugees fleeing the mainland and entry permits were hard to get. I was also told not to say a word because I only spoke Mandarin, the national language of China, not Cantonese, which was spoken in parts of southern China and Hong Kong. I refused to cut my hair, wear a straw hat, or remove my glasses, but I did agree to let my traveling companions speak for me.

偷
渡
到
香
港

Opposite foreground:
This is the travel permit my mother obtained for me in July 1950 to travel from Shanghai to Guangzhou, the city on the Chinese mainland closest to Hong Kong.

Opposite background:
In 1950 Hong Kong was a huge city with millions of residents. Although I had sneaked in without a permit, I soon realized I would never be discovered and sent back to China.

51

At the border there was an area called No Man's Land where we were taken into one of two tents—one for males and the other for females—and were thoroughly searched. The contents of my suitcase were dumped out onto a table. Officials looked at my Bible and I was afraid that it might be taken away. I told them it was the only one I had and was for my own use, and they let me keep it. As my handbag was searched, I became really frightened! But my Chinese Nationalist passport was not found. My mother, in her wisdom, had sewn it between the cover and stiff lining of my handbag. We were afraid that if it was found the Communist officials might have prevented me from leaving China. When the officials flipped through my diaries, they found only writings about family and schooldays, so they gave them back to me.

We then proceeded to the river that divided the Chinese mainland from the Kowloon Peninsula, which was part of Hong Kong. It was a chaotic situation, with a big crowd of people pushing and fighting to get across the bridge over the river into British territory. By the time I got to the bridge, my companions had already made it across. There, an officer was checking the entrance permit of each person. "Your permit?" he asked me when I got to the front of the line. I just stood there, stunned, because I did not have a permit to enter Hong Kong. Suddenly an idea came to my mind. I hurriedly tore open my handbag, took out my passport, and showed it to the officer. "I'll only be in Hong Kong for a short while before I leave for the United States to enter college," I said. Still, he refused to let me cross. I felt like a person reaching heaven's gate but not allowed entry, and I just stood there not knowing what to do. Then, as the officer's attention was diverted to other people in the crowd, I heard a man behind me saying, "Run! This is your chance!" Once I heard him say that, I didn't give his words a second thought or even pause to look back to see who had spoken. I just picked up my little suitcase and ran as fast as I could across the bridge.

On the other side, parallel to the river, there was a railroad track on which a train was standing. I ran around the front of the train to the other side. I crouched down and looked under the train to see if anybody was coming after me. I waited there for a few minutes, watching. When I was assured that nobody was chasing me, I went to find the family I was traveling with. They were waiting for me near a little store and helped me get on a bus to go to the Hillwood Road Baptist Church, where my sister had stayed a year earlier.

That was how I got into Hong Kong. Years later I would jokingly tell friends that I sneaked into Hong Kong, which actually was the truth! At first, I was apprehensive that I might be discovered living there without a permit and would be sent back to China. But after some time I realized that I was completely lost among Hong Kong's millions of residents!

When I got to the church I met my father's friend Rev. Zhong Enguang (鍾恩光), who already had been notified of my arrival. This young pastor's little family, which included his wife and a baby boy, was living in a corner of the church balcony that was enclosed by a curtain. There was nowhere they could house me, so I slept on a church pew for a few weeks and ate meals with them in the church's kitchen downstairs. I sent my expired passport to Taiwan to be renewed, and after I finally got it back I applied for my visa from the American Consulate. While waiting for my visa, I moved into a small room in a hotel not far from the church. The room held only a narrow bed and a little table and chair. The wall separating my room and the room next door did not reach the ceiling, and deep into the night I struggled to fall asleep due to the loud noise made by my neighbors playing mahjong, a gambling game. It was a

terrible place! For breakfast and lunch, I ate saltine crackers and drank powdered milk, which I bought and mixed with water. My suppers I ate with the pastor's family.

At the church, I met a girl about my age named Gan Xingkui (甘杏葵), whom we called Lydia Kan. She was in Hong Kong for the summer attending Bible school and working with local children's and women's programs. Her friendship helped to lessen my loneliness and homesickness, and we became lifelong friends. In the early evenings after Lydia came

Rev. Zhong Enguang, pastor of the Hillwood Road Baptist Church, and his wife took me in when I first arrived in Hong Kong. Conditions were so crowded that I had to sleep on a church pew. Here they are with their baby boy.

53

Top: My friendship with Gan Xingkui (left), whom we called Lydia Kan, made me feel less homesick when I was in Hong Kong.

Bottom: Although I had refused to cut off my braids before entering Hong Kong, I decided to do so before leaving for the United States.

home from work, we would rent bicycles and ride on the sidewalks near the church. Sometimes she took me with her to visit her aunt who lived on an island near Hong Kong. To get there, we had to travel by boat and train. That was where I saw a famous landmark, a natural stone formation on top of a mountain that resembled a mother carrying a child on her back. It was said that the woman's husband had left home to find work but never returned. The woman climbed the mountain to wait for him. A sad story!

Lydia had to go back to school in September, and I missed spending time with her very much. One day while I was in my little hotel room, I had a visitor named Han Chengxin (韓誠信) who went by the name Daniel Han. He was the son of a colleague of my father's from Kaifeng. He was about eight years older than I and was like a big brother to me. I was very happy to see him! He had heard that I had come to Hong Kong and found out where I was staying. When he saw my room he said, "This is not where you should be. I live north of here, where there are better rooms for rent." So I moved there until I was able to leave for the United States. About a week or two before I left Hong Kong, I decided to have my braids cut off. Although long, braided hair had been the custom when I was growing up, by 1950 short hair was getting more popular. It was also much easier to take care of!

Chapter 11

ON A SLOW BOAT TO AMERICA

When my father got word that I was ready to leave Hong Kong, he booked passage for me, not on an airplane, but on the USS *General Gordon*, which I called the Slow Boat to America! On October 17, 1950, after I had been in Hong Kong for about three and a half months, Rev. and Mrs. Victor Frank, a missionary couple who were friends of my father's, took me to the boat dock and saw me off. Due to the state of my health, my father had bought me a first-class ticket. In first class, the passengers were treated royally, and the food was fabulous! But most of the time I was seasick and couldn't eat much. Before I left Hong Kong I had been told that eating pickles would help, but even though I tried to eat them every day, it did not. Sometimes the boat rocked so much that all I could do was lie in my bunk.

Because I was traveling in first class, I did not meet most of the Chinese students on the ship. I did meet one Chinese girl I thought was a student. I later found out she was going to the United States to get married. The tenth day of the Pacific Ocean crossing happened to be my twentieth birthday, October 29. On that day, we crossed the International Date Line, so I had two birthdays that year!

We reached San Francisco on November 4. When we passed under the Golden Gate Bridge I was really excited. The bridge was known to those of us emigrating to the United States as The Gate to America, and I was, indeed, in America! But, alas, I was not permitted to disembark because I did not have the right documents. I was scared and did not know what to do. Sometime later, a man came aboard and asked for me. A stranger to me, but another friend of my father's, he introduced himself as Rev. Chee Wu, pastor of a Baptist church in San Francisco. He had been notified of my arrival and wanted to meet me. When he found out I was not allowed to disembark, he got permission to board the ship. But he couldn't take me to his home because I was to be detained in the immigration building until officials clarified my status. In this detention building we were divided by nationality and then placed into separate rooms for men and women. But we

漫渡到美國

Opposite top: My ticket for first-class passage from Hong Kong to San Francisco on the USS General Gordon cost my parents $400.

Opposite middle: I was very excited, and nervous, as I finally left for America.

Opposite bottom: An American missionary couple, Rev. and Mrs. Victor Frank, saw me off when I sailed on October 17, 1950.

I met this lovely Chinese girl on the USS General Gordon. She was sailing to the United States to get married.

all went to the same dining hall for meals. There, we lined up like prisoners to get our trays and waited for the people serving the food to dish it out for us. I disliked the food immensely but forced myself to eat.

We lived in large, dormitory-like rooms, but my roommates were mostly Cantonese or from the southeastern coastal regions of China, and didn't speak Mandarin. Because I didn't understand their dialects, we couldn't communicate, and so, to pass the time, I visited the detention center's small library to browse for books. My English was poor, but I had my English–Chinese dictionary with me and I used it to try to read. I found a book called *The King's General*, written by Daphne du Maurier. I started reading it, and although I struggled, it turned out to be an interesting story. However, I was only able to read a few pages

before I was released from the detention center. Years later, I was visiting my parents in College Park, Maryland. On one of my walks I went into a used bookstore where I found a copy of *The King's General*. I was very happy and bought it so I could finish reading the story. I read it again, a second time, years later.

On November 11, my status was cleared up and I was allowed to leave the detention center. The Baptist pastor saw me off on a plane headed to Louisville, Kentucky. When I arrived at the airport terminal my father was not there, but I was met by several ladies who told me that he was at a meeting and had asked them to welcome me. I was taken by a Mrs. Graham (no relation to the evangelist Billy Graham, whom I would, however, soon see) to her home, where I stayed for nearly a month. She was a widow and lived in a small house by herself. I remember that every morning after I got out of bed I would feel the floor moving. The effect of the ocean crossing had affected me that much! For breakfast, Mrs. Graham would often have grapefruit. She told me it was good for me, but it tasted so sour that even with sugar on it I could hardly eat it. She was very kind and loving, and I really enjoyed knowing her.

My father finally returned to Louisville and I was very happy to see him.

Soon we were off in his small car, stopping first in Hodgenville, Kentucky, the birthplace of President Abraham Lincoln. We then drove to see Lois, who by now was attending Carson-Newman College in Jefferson City, Tennessee. It was so good to see her again after having been separated for a year and a half! A few days later, my father and I drove to Atlanta, Georgia, to visit a retired missionary, Miss Blanche Walker, with whom my father had worked at the Baptist Publication House in Shanghai in the early 1930s. She took us to hear Billy Graham, who was conducting a revival meeting in a big tent. I could only understand a few words, like *Jesus* and *Bible*. Miss Walker also took us to see the Atlanta Cyclorama & Civil War Museum, a giant building housing a circular painting named the *Battle of Atlanta*. The painting was surrounded by a round walkway with a railing. Although I didn't know anything about American history at the time, it was quite something to see. I remember looking down from the walkway at the lifelike soldiers, some fallen and covered in blood. It looked like a real battlefield. Then my father and I drove to Stone Mountain, a city near Atlanta to see the images of three Civil War Confederate heroes: President Jefferson Davis and Generals Robert E. Lee and Thomas

J. "Stonewall" Jackson etched into the side of a mountain. It was a gigantic undertaking that was not quite finished.

After the Atlanta visit, we went to Memphis, Tennessee, to visit my father's friends, Charles and Minnie Carter. They had made arrangements for me to enter the nearby Oakville Memorial Sanatorium. We stayed with the Carters for a few days and went to their church on the Sunday

Top: Soon after I arrived in the United States my father and I visited Hodgenville, Kentucky, birthplace of President Abraham Lincoln.

Bottom: Our next stop was to visit Lois, who was a student at Carson-Newman College in Jefferson City, Tennessee.

Top: Because I needed further treatment for my tuberculosis, I entered Oakville Memorial Sanatorium just outside of Memphis, Tennessee. I would stay there for a year and a half.

Middle: When I first arrived at the sanatorium I missed my family so much that I cried every night. But soon I got to know some of the other, younger patients and things got better.

Bottom: Here I am with Mary Lynn Britt (center), one of my best friends at the sanatorium, and Laura Baker Jones (right), a friend who visited me on Sunday afternoons.

before I was admitted to the sanatorium. That day, in the church's Sunday school class for women, I met Laura Baker Jones, a lady who became a lifelong friend. Laura came to visit me at the sanatorium every Sunday afternoon and helped me learn English. She also taught me to crochet and to play the ukulele that she bought for me. Mrs. Carter came to see me nearly every Wednesday afternoon.

At the sanatorium, I stayed at first in a room with several patients who were much older than I, and I was very lonely. I missed my family so much that I cried nearly every night. Over time, things got better. First, I was moved to another room with younger patients closer to my age. Then, a girl was brought in who was a little younger than I, and our beds were placed next to each other. Her name was Mary Lynn Britt. We became close friends and still communicate with each other all these years later. Another girl who was four years older than I, Anne Scott, came a little later, and we quickly became lifelong friends, too. She passed away a few years ago.

One of the physicians at the sanatorium was Dr. Eleanor Soltau, who had been born and raised in South Korea by her American missionary parents. Like me, she had contracted tuberculosis as a child, later coming to the United States to attend college and medical school. She was single, tall, slender, and very attractive. We all loved and admired her. I especially loved it when she seemed to linger just slightly longer at my bedside than at the other patients'. There was an older doctor on the staff who was not tall, but round in the middle, very jolly, and very lovable. Among ourselves, we called him Santa Claus.

After I had been in the sanatorium for some time, the doctors decided to give me "air shots," which involved using a big needle to force air into my abdomen beneath my diaphragm to keep my lungs from expanding and help them heal faster. I also went through a procedure in which the phrenic nerve controlling the movements of the lungs was cut slightly but not severed. I still have a faint scar on my neck from the procedure, which I underwent twice. In the summer of 1952, after a year and a half in the sanatorium, I was discharged. I was told my TB was *arrested*, and that I was no longer contagious. Mrs. Carter arranged a train ride for me to Washington, DC, where my father and Lois were living. My father had bought a little row house at 3310 Nineteenth Street, in the northwest section of

the city, in anticipation of the arrival of my mother and brothers. He was working at the US State Department as a translator and selling cookware door to door, part time. I remember that when the train passed the Capitol, I thought it was the White House. That spring I lived with my father, but took the bus to George Washington University Hospital where I continued my treatments.

Dr. Eleanor Soltau was one of the most popular doctors at the sanatorium.

61

Chapter 12
COLLEGE LIFE

On June 7, 1952, my father received a cable from Hong Kong. It was from my mother saying she and my brothers had arrived there from Shanghai on June 1. We were so happy and thankful, and immediately knelt down to thank God. They would, however, be forced to stay in Hong Kong for another six and a half months before they could get all the documents needed to travel to the United States. My grandmother, we learned, had decided to stay in Shanghai with my cousin, telling my mother she felt too old to travel any farther.

While we waited for the rest of our family to come to America, I was at last able to begin my college education. Even before I left China, I knew that eventually I would attend Mary Hardin-Baylor College (MH-BC), a Southern Baptist college for women, just as Auntie Zemma had wished. The first college for women west of the Mississippi, MH-BC was founded in 1845 in Independence, Texas. Then it was known as Baylor Female College, the female department of Baylor University. It moved to Belton, about forty

miles south of Waco, in 1866, and in 1934 changed its name to honor its biggest benefactor. (Today, it is known as the University of Mary Hardin-Baylor.) Auntie Zemma's dear friend, Mrs. Minnie Lott, also of Orange, Texas, had been writing me letters about the college while I was growing up in Kaifeng. Even though I struggled to answer her letters in my broken English, she never gave up on me. Finally, in the fall of 1952, I was able to apply for entrance and was accepted. My father knew a family who attended our church in Washington whose daughter, Dolores Rannings, was attending MH-BC. Her parents were very kind, and allowed me to travel with them all the way to Belton, a two-day drive from Washington, when they took Dolores to school. There were no superhighways at the time, and I got to see much of the country.

In my freshman year, I made two lifetime friends. One was La Niece Robison, from Fort Worth, Texas, and the other was my roommate, Janet Pritz, from Albuquerque, New Mexico. On one spring break I was invited to La Niece's home, and another

大學生涯

Opposite foreground: My years at Mary Hardin-Baylor College were very happy ones.

Opposite background: Mary Hardin-Baylor College was founded in 1845 as the first college west of the Mississippi for women.

Top: My classmate La Niece Robison, from Fort Worth, Texas, became a lifelong friend.

Bottom: During freshman initiation, my friend Jenny Ling (left) and I wore tubes made out of rolled-up paper in our hair.

time, to Janet's. Janet's father took us to the Carlsbad Cavern. It was truly amazing! One weekend in my freshman year I was invited to Mr. and Mrs. Lott's home in Orange. They showed me the pickling plant they owned, a giant operation that I found quite interesting and educational. They also took me to the cemetery where Auntie Zemma was buried.

As a freshman, I took the basic required subjects. My favorite subjects were English literature and general science. In English literature, we were assigned books such as *The Canterbury Tales* by Chaucer, *Paradise Lost* by Milton, and *The Return of the Native* by Thomas Hardy. (Years later, I happened to see a copy of *The Return of the Native* at a used book sale. I bought it and read it again.) We also studied poems such as *The Rime of the Ancient Mariner* by Samuel Taylor Coleridge and "We Are Seven" by William Wordsworth, which was about a girl, the only girl among seven siblings, who had lost her sister. I could really relate to this poem because there had been seven of us, and I had lost a sister. Because I didn't know English very well I had to use the dictionary quite frequently, but with much struggle I was able to pass the exam.

While in college, I stayed in Stribling Hall, one of the three dormitories

on campus. Girls from MH-BC who were dating boys from Texas A&M University at College Station, about ninety miles away, had to be back on campus every night by nine o'clock. I had one date with a Chinese A&M student. We didn't really hit it off and I don't even remember his name. I do remember that we were required to wear skirts or dresses to class, but slacks and blue jeans were allowed elsewhere on campus. As a freshman, I bought my first pair of jeans. I liked them very much.

I decided to attend summer school after my freshman year to speed up my education. I took an English course, a class on the Bible, and Introduction to Sociology. I liked the first two, but I didn't learn much in the sociology class, mostly because neither the professor nor the subject was very interesting. However, the weather was the worst part of summer school. I had not considered how hot it would be in southern Texas in the summer! The heat was almost unbearable, mostly because I was not used to it. In the early evenings, when it was cooler, we had vesper services on a grassy slope outside our dormitory. One night I was sitting behind another girl and saw something crawling on the back of her shirt. In the twilight, I could just make out that it was a scorpion. I told her not to move and then brushed it off and killed it in the grass. The scorpion bite is very

Here I am in the spring of 1953 sitting on the steps of my dormitory, Stribling Hall, wearing my first pair of blue jeans.

65

painful and lasts a long time. I knew that because once in China I had been bitten on my finger by a scorpion.

One night in my sophomore year, while sleeping in my dorm room, I was awakened by a scratching noise made by a little mouse. I didn't know how it had gotten into my room, but it was disrupting my sleep so I decided to devise a method to catch it. I turned my wastepaper basket upside down, propped up one side with a book, and placed a piece of bread underneath. When the mouse went in to eat the bread, I caught it, and put it in a little glass jar with holes in the lid. The next day I took it to my science class, taught by a bachelor, Dr. York, and put it on his desk. I wrote him a note to indicate this was a live specimen for his collection from me. He wasn't very amused!

My sophomore year I had to declare a major and a minor. I thought about majoring in English literature, which I liked very much, but I knew that after graduation I would have to find work. If I majored in English literature, I realized, I would have to get a master's, and perhaps even a doctoral, degree. I decided instead to focus on science, which I also liked. In fact, as a young girl I had dreamed of being a doctor. I later changed my mind because of a lack of self-confidence as well as all the

time I had lost recovering from tuberculosis. However, I decided to major in biology and minor in chemistry. I joined the science club and was elected president. Once, the club went to a seminar at Texas A&M University with our professors. There I learned about different occupations in science. To become a lab technician I would need to take a one-year course and complete a one-year internship in a hospital lab. To become a medical technologist, I would need to get a bachelor of science degree, which would take four years, and complete a one-year internship. I decided to become a medical technologist, but finished my degree in three years because of my summer school work.

To graduate, we had to study one foreign language and take one elective class. I decided on French and Music Appreciation. I really enjoyed the Music Appreciation class. One of the campus buildings, Presser Hall, was for music courses only. That was where our lectures, mostly about classical music, took place. We were required to learn about the composers and the pieces they composed, and to recognize the different movements in their compositions. I remember listening to recordings of those compositions over and over in small rooms in Presser Hall that were equipped with record players. It was not easy!

I remember several of my professors very well. My Bible professor, Dr. William Sisk, and my father were good friends who had met at Southwestern Baptist Theological Seminary in Fort Worth, Texas, in the early 1930s. Dr. and Mrs. Sisk lived near campus and they invited me for supper several times. I attended the First Baptist Church, the same church they attended, which was within walking distance of my dorm. One year an excellent English professor at MH-BC, Dr. Vann, taught the Sunday school class for the seniors. Unfortunately, because I was not a senior at the time, I could not take his class.

One of my English professors was a single lady who was quite severe and much feared. I remember that once she called on a girl to go to the blackboard and diagram a sentence. The girl couldn't do it and was reprimanded right in front of the class. The girl started to cry and I developed a great dislike of this professor!

My chemistry professor, Dr. Gertrude Vermillion, seemed to take an interest in me and invited me to her home more than once for supper. She was not married and had no family nearby. One time, I cooked a Chinese meal for her. However, I didn't know much about cooking, so it wasn't anything to be proud of! I remember that

one evening, needing to finish a chemistry experiment for Dr. Vermillion's class, I went to the chemistry lab on the third floor of the Wells Science Hall. I was the only one there. Suddenly a strong wind shook the whole building.

Dr. Gertrude Vermillion, my chemistry professor, invited me to her home, where I once cooked her a Chinese meal.

The next day I found out that a tornado had passed through the town of Waco, about forty miles north of campus. A few days later, a professor drove me and a few other students to Waco to view the devastation. It reminded me of the bombing in my hometown of Kaifeng.

I studied European history, but was also interested in knowing something of American history. In China, we had learned a little about two famous American presidents, George Washington and Abraham Lincoln. I was especially interested in Lincoln, so on my own I checked out a library book titled *Love Is Eternal* by Irving Stone, which told the story of Lincoln, his wife, Mary Todd, and their family. I enjoyed reading this book very much. By the time I was a sophomore, my English was much better, but I was not quite a fluent speaker. Later, I enjoyed reading books

67

about Russian history, and bought *Nicholas and Alexandra* by Robert K. Massie, the story of Czar Nicholas II and his family during the Russian Revolution of 1917. I also read *Doctor Zhivago* by Boris Pasternak. After college, I belonged to a book club for several years, and gradually accumulated a good collection of books.

Outside of class, I was busy. I joined the Baptist Student Union as a freshman and remained a member the entire time I was in school. Once, we attended a BSU convention in San Antonio, where we visited the Alamo. I also was in the college's prison ministry, and with other students visited women prisoners many Sunday

afternoons, sharing the Gospel message with them. We also invited local Mexican children to attend Bible story time. In April 1955, we took them on an outing to the outskirts of campus where we crossed Nolan Creek to view the high cliffs of a nearby mountain.

College was a very enjoyable experience for me, and almost all my memories are pleasant—except for my trips freshman year to what was then Scott and White Memorial Hospital. At the time, the hospital, which was nine miles northeast of Belton in Temple, was one of the most well known in the South. Every three weeks I had to skip breakfast

and walk to the bus station just off campus and catch the early morning bus to the hospital. There I waited to be called, sometimes for many hours, to receive additional air shots. When I returned to school it was usually late afternoon and I would have missed not just breakfast, but also lunch. I always felt very full, bloated, and miserable after this treatment and couldn't eat anyway. I would lie down and try to take a nap. The whole day's classes had been missed! By the end of freshman year, the doctors told me that I didn't need any more treatments. I was very thankful!

I finished my coursework at MH-BC in the spring of 1955, but would not receive my BS degree until I completed a year of internship in a hospital laboratory.

Through the Baptist Student Union, I helped run Bible classes for local Mexican children. In April 1955, my classmates and I (back row, far right) took the children on a fieldtrip to nearby Nolan Creek.

Chapter 13

OUR FAMILY REUNION

Shortly after Christmas 1952, during my freshman year in college, my mother cabled my father to tell him she and my brothers had booked passage from Hong Kong to San Francisco on the SS *President Cleveland*. They were to sail on January 13, 1953. Two days later, my father started driving to San Francisco. He stopped first in Jefferson City, Tennessee, where he stayed with his friends Dr. and Mrs. Warden for the night before driving the next morning to Carson-Newman College to have breakfast with Lois. His next stop was Memphis, where he spent the night with the Carters before driving to El Dorado, Arkansas, to stay with Rev. Carl A. Clark, his wife, Mayola, and their two daughters. "Uncle" Carl and my father had been schoolmates at Southwestern Baptist Theological Seminary and were still close friends. In fact, Lois and I had just spent the Christmas holiday with him and his family. While my father was staying with the Clarks he preached at their church, Immanuel Baptist. His sermon was titled "Preach, Praise, Pray, and Practice." That evening, he gave testimony about his life and love story at a church in Smackover, about twelve miles from El Dorado. (Two days later, on Tuesday, January 20, Dwight D. Eisenhower, the new president of the United States, was inaugurated.) After staying with the Clarks for a few days to rest and speak at a school and several other churches nearby, my father drove on to Belton, Texas. There, he stayed with the family of my Bible professor, Dr. Sisk, and visited with me.

On the evening of January 27, he arrived in Bakersfield, California, where he went to a Chinese restaurant and met the owner and his family. The next day, he drove all the way to San Francisco, where he had dinner with his friend, Rev. Chee Wu, and his family. It was Rev. Wu who had met me when I arrived in San Francisco two years earlier. That night my father stayed in a YMCA; he would have to wait three more days for my mother and brothers to arrive. At one point, he had to go to the US Immigration Office on business. But as he set off, he discovered that he had lost his wristwatch. He searched everywhere and couldn't find

閤家團圓

Opposite foreground: Our family reunion in February 1953 at the home of Rev. Carl A. Clark and his wife, Mayola, was a joyous occasion. Back row, left to right: Lois, Samuel, Joseph, and me. Front row, left to right: James, my mother, my father, and Eugene.

Opposite background: Those of us who emigrated to the United States called San Francisco's Golden Gate Bridge the Gate to America.

Rev. Carl Clark and my father had been schoolmates at Southwestern Baptist Theological Seminary and remained close friends the rest of their lives. Here are "Uncle" Carl, his wife, Mayola, and their daughters, Jennie (left) and Claudia, at their El Dorado, Arkansas, home.

it, so he gave up. After coming back to where he had parked his car five hours earlier, he looked for his watch again and found it on the edge of the sidewalk. It was there in plain sight, and it was a miracle that nobody else had seen it! He was very thankful.

Over the next two days my father met friends from the Golden Gate Baptist Seminary and attended meetings, where one speaker spoke on "The Challenge of Missions." While waiting in San Francisco, my father received a check for twenty-five dollars in the mail from Miss Jean Morrison,

a friend who attended church with him in Washington, DC. I remember my father telling us how grateful he was for her help and thoughtfulness. I met Miss Morrison one summer in Washington when I was home from college.

My mother and four brothers finally arrived in San Francisco on Saturday, January 31, 1953. After a separation of six and a half years, and with the wide Pacific Ocean between them, it is not hard to imagine the scene of their joyful reunion! That night there was a welcoming party at one of San Francisco's Baptist churches where my father had preached in the past. On Sunday, he preached three times: in the morning in a church in Oakland, that afternoon at Chinese Independence Baptist Church, and in the evening at a San Francisco Baptist center. On Monday my parents and brothers continued their celebration by touring the San Francisco Zoo at Golden Gate Park before packing for their trip back to Washington.

On the morning of February 5, they left San Francisco, heading east. But after only 167 miles, in Mariposa, California, their car developed trouble and had to be fixed. They had to spend the night in a motel, where they took two rooms that cost three dollars each. The next day they left Mariposa, touring a small part of nearby Yosemite National Park before traveling through Fresno, Bakersfield, and Barstow to Needles, California, where they stayed the night. Over the next week they drove through Arizona and New Mexico on their way to visit me in Belton. In Texas, my father spoke at the Westside Baptist Church in Plainview and visited Chinese missionaries in Dallas.

They arrived in Belton on February 12. I remember that the housemother in my dormitory called me and said, "Your family is here!" I ran out to meet them, and my mother and I both started crying.

My brothers had grown much taller, and were very happy to see me. We had dinner together in the dining hall, where my family met Dr. Louise Blunt, the dean of women. She was tall and very stately, and highly respected. However, to me, she had always seemed very severe. Yet after she spent time talking with my family and hearing some of their stories, I noticed tears in her eyes. That was when I realized that she really had a very soft heart.

While in Belton, my parents and brothers stayed first with the Sisks and then in a guesthouse on campus. They visited friends

Lois and I spent Christmas 1952 with the Clarks. Here she is (on roller skates) with Jennie (left, also on skates) and Claudia.

Once my brothers were living in Washington, DC, and going to school, they all got part-time jobs delivering newspapers. Here I am with James (left) and Joseph in Rock Creek Park, Washington, DC, in 1954.

other again, our reunion was a wonderful, momentous event. Although Lois and I had to return to school after a few days, my parents and brothers stayed with the Clarks for about two weeks while my father preached at churches in the area. The boys stayed in a bedroom above the Clarks' garage, where Joseph listened to a set of Bozo the Clown records over and over.

While there, we spoke among ourselves in Chinese. I remember one conversation in which we used the phrase *mei you le*, meaning "no more" (as in "having run out of something") several times. Mayola Clark overheard us and wondered why we were mentioning her name, which was pronounced the same way. She laughed at my explanation, and after that we endearingly started calling her "Auntie No More," which she got a kick out of and didn't mind at all. Oh, how I miss her and Uncle Carl!

The six of us were traveling in a 1950 two-door, black Chevy, its roof piled so high with luggage that at one motel, a suitcase hit the vacancy sign. When we got to Nashville, we dropped Samuel off at Belmont College. Fresh off the boat and barely nineteen years old, I wonder how he must have felt, thrust into an entirely new environment. Was he fearful, anxious or eager? Did he have language problems? We'll never know. He graduated from

in the area and relaxed after their long trip. I remember my father wrote some letters and preached at the Immanuel Baptist Church in nearby Temple. After a few days they all traveled to Fort Worth and toured Southwestern Baptist Theological Seminary, returning briefly to Belton before leaving for Orange, Texas, to visit friends and the grave of Auntie Zemma. Although I was sad to see them go, we met up again a few days later at the Clarks' in El Dorado. With Lois traveling there as well, we held a true family reunion.

After having been separated for so long and worried that we might never see each

Belmont in 1957, entered Vanderbilt University's School of Medicine, and in 1961 earned his MD.

Soon after the rest of my family arrived in Washington, my three youngest brothers started going to school. To help with expenses they got part-time jobs delivering newspapers. My mother worked at a dressmaking shop, sewing and making alterations. With everyone pitching in, my family was never dependent on the government for benefits—something that made my parents proud.

With my entire family finally living in Washington, I felt for the first time as if I had a real home in this country. How wonderful it was to have a place to spend my summers during college! We lived near Rock Creek Park, which borders the National Zoo, and one of our most enjoyable pastimes was to go to the zoo on outings. (In fact, we lived so close to the zoo that in the middle of the night we could sometimes hear the lions roar and the elephants trumpet!) The zoo was a vast place, so each time we visited we would tour a different area trying not to get lost. We frequently went to the National Mall and toured the museums and galleries: the Smithsonian Castle, the National Gallery

Left: My brothers (left to right) Joseph, James, and Eugene in the summer of 1954, standing in front of a statue of Marquis de Lafayette. That summer I ate my dinner sitting on a bench near the statue on my way to a night class at George Washington University.

Right: A few years later, in 1959, the oldest of my four brothers, Samuel, was studying for his MD degree at Vanderbilt University after graduating from Belmont College—both in Nashville, Tennessee.

Here I am in 1954 in College Park, Maryland, in the yard of one of my parents' friends.

driving to the conference through the Great Smoky and Blue Ridge Mountains, where the scenery was quite spectacular, and being able to truly appreciate the lyrics to the song "America the Beautiful"!

We had to cut short our attendance at the conference because of Lois's need to exchange her visiting student visa for a Permanent Resident Card before her twenty-first birthday. At the time, the only way for her to do so was to leave and then re-enter the United States under her new status. Lois decided to travel to Cuba, where it was discovered that, according to her passport, she was already twenty-one. That was because of the traditional Chinese custom of considering newborns a year old at birth and adding one year to their age each New Year's Day. So, we all had to return to Washington, where my father showed immigration officials our family Bible, in which he had recorded the birth dates of all his children. They then contacted the American Consulate in Cuba, where Lois's date of birth was corrected and her Permanent Resident Card issued.

The following summer, back home in Washington, I decided to take Anatomy—which was required for my degree—in the evenings at George Washington University. But I also wanted a part-time summer job to help with expenses. I searched the want

of Art, the Museum of Natural History, and the Air and Space Museum. We also climbed the Washington Monument, and visited the Lincoln Memorial, the Jefferson Memorial, the Capitol, and the Library of Congress. Living in Washington was not only enjoyable, but also educational. I recall the years my family spent there as happy ones.

It was during the summer of 1953, after I attended summer school at MH-BC, that my family took a trip to attend a gathering of Southern Baptist missionaries, pastoral workers, and their families at the Ridgecrest Conference Center in the mountains of North Carolina. I remember ads of the *Washington Post*, saw that the American Research Bureau was hiring, and sent in my resume. I thought the job would be in medical or scientific research and was happy, thinking it might be something related to my studies. But when I was called for an interview I found out that the position was neither; instead, it involved surveying the American people's television viewing habits! I was somewhat disappointed, but decided that a job was a job. I was hired at minimum wage, which at the time was seventy-five cents an hour, mostly to mimeograph documents and stuff envelopes. I remember bringing a sandwich to have for supper after work, and eating it sitting on a bench under a statue of Marquis de Lafayette located just north of the White House. Then I would go to class, getting out after dark to take the bus home. Often, I was the only one waiting at the bus stop, which was across the street from the White House. That summer, Lois got a job as a waitress at the local Hot Shoppes restaurant. I remember that when she came home from work we would sit at our dining room table counting her tips.

I have fond memories of several trips I made to the Washington area years later to visit my parents, who by then were living in a little house in nearby College Park, Maryland. On one trip, I was reunited with my good friend from high school, Hannah Du, who had traveled to the United States to minister in a Lutheran church in New York State. By coincidence, Hannah had followed much the same journey as I had, living first in Shanghai while attending a Lutheran Bible school and then working as a missionary near Hong Kong. We had visited each other in Shanghai and in Hong Kong, and when bidding me farewell as I left for the United States, she said, "We will probably never see each other again." But, to my delight, we did. What's more, we remained close for many years. Hannah later moved permanently to New York City, where she lived for a long time before her death, which was not long ago.

Another time, I decided to travel from College Park to explore Washington by myself. I bought a round-trip bus ticket and a map of Washington, got on the bus early in the morning, and stayed until the museums closed. That was the day I discovered a place I had never known before: the National Portrait Gallery. I recall it as a wonderful day. I just felt so happy and free!

Chapter 14
MEETING A STRANGER

One day in January 1954, during my sophomore year of college, I received a letter from a stranger by the name of Tsu-Ming Han (韓祖銘, Han Zuming), a doctoral student in geology at the University of Minnesota, in Minneapolis. I was very curious and opened it. The Chinese handwriting was quite beautiful and the letter was written in such a way that I was very impressed. I could tell right away that Tsu-Ming was a scholar. In the letter, he introduced himself and said that like me, he was from Henan Province. He said he had learned about me from a fellow student at the University of Minnesota named Lincoln Liu who knew my father and that he had a daughter in college in Texas. Tsu-Ming said he wished that I would answer him. I did, and we became pen pals. I still have all his letters. Later, Tsu-Ming asked me for a photograph of myself. I only had one—which I didn't like—of me standing alone by a tree. I sent it to him anyway. He sent me a framed portrait of himself.

Tsu-Ming Han was born on September 11, 1924, the oldest of five children, in the small, remote, rural village of Sha-Chu Zin in central Henan Province. Life was hard for the Han family. Their home was primitive—built into the side of a hill—and they grew almost all their own food. It was also, at times, dangerous. When only a little boy, Tsu-Ming was kidnapped and held for fifty-five days by bandits demanding a ransom. At one point, they threatened to cut off his ear. The ransom was a stack of silver coins as tall as he, amounting to five hundred Chinese dollars. Tsu-Ming's father was the first person in his family to graduate from high school. He became a teacher and later started his own school. Tsu-Ming's mother never went to school, yet like her husband, she believed in the importance of education. Because there was no high school in their village, Tsu-Ming attended high school in Kaifeng and went on to earn a bachelor's degree at Northwest University at Xi'an.

An excellent student, Tsu-Ming qualified to be sent by the Chinese Nationalist government to the United States for further education. He traveled to the states in December 1947, on the USS *General*

一位陌生人的萍水相逢

Opposite foreground: This is the photo I sent to Tsu-Ming Han after we had been corresponding for a while. I didn't like it, but it was the only one I had.

Opposite background: Tsu-Ming Han was a doctoral student at the University of Minnesota when he first wrote to me in January 1954.

Top: Tsu-Ming Han was a college student in Xi'an when, in 1947, he was chosen by the Chinese Nationalist government to study abroad in the United States.

Bottom: Tsu-Ming received his master's degree in geology from the University of Cincinnati in 1949.

Gordon, the same ship on which I had made the trip. There, despite his poor English, Tsu-Ming was admitted to graduate school at the University of Cincinnati, where he earned a master's degree in geology in 1949. It wasn't easy. There were many times Tsu-Ming didn't understand his professors' lectures, and he found writing papers and taking exams difficult. Still, he liked the congenial atmosphere at the university and had planned to stay on to earn a PhD. By then, however, the Communists had taken over China and Tsu-Ming lost his scholarship. There he was, a twenty-four-year-old, penniless student in America. Somehow, he got to know two other Chinese students who were in the same situation. They heard of a Jewish children's camp in New York City that was hiring workers, traveled there, and got jobs as dishwashers.

At the end of the summer, Tsu-Ming's advisor, Dr. John Rich, recommended that Tsu-Ming transfer to the University of Minnesota, which had a stronger doctoral program in economic geology, Tsu-Ming's field of study, than the University of Cincinnati. He was able to cover his expenses with a scholarship from the university and a part-time job at the US Bureau of Mines in Minneapolis. Unfortunately, he found the University of Minnesota much less enjoyable than the University of Cincinnati. Yet

he completed the coursework for his PhD and passed his written doctoral exams. He took a summer job in the research laboratory of the Cleveland-Cliffs Iron Company in Ishpeming, Michigan, a mining company working to upgrade the quality of iron ore so that it could be used in the steel industry. Tsu-Ming's supervisors liked him so much they offered him a permanent job, which he agreed to take after finishing school.

Back at the University of Minnesota, Tsu-Ming went to work on his dissertation. However, much to his dismay, he failed his oral exams, largely because of his poor spoken English, which had not been taken into consideration. Dr. Rich thought that was unfair and offered to help Tsu-Ming find an alternative route to his PhD, but died before that could happen. Meanwhile, Tsu-Ming left the university with a master's degree in economic geology and took a position as a microscopist at Cleveland-Cliffs.

Tsu-Ming had written to me about Ishpeming, then a small city of almost

Tsu-Ming enjoyed the time he spent at the University of Cincinnati. Here he is (back row, far left), with some of his fellow students, and one of their professors visiting the Great Smoky Mountains in 1948.

Ishpeming, Mich.

Tsu-Ming took a part-time, summer job at the Cleveland-Cliffs Iron Company in Ishpeming, Michigan, while he was in graduate school at the University of Minnesota. The word Ishpeming *means "high ground" in the language of the Indians who settled the area.*

nine thousand people that had been settled by immigrants—including many from Finland—coming to work in the mines. The word *Ishpeming* means "high ground" in the language of the Native Americans who had settled the area, a reference to the city's location on a ridge of land between Lake Superior and Lake Michigan. Actually, even before going to work at Cleveland-Cliffs, Ishpeming was familiar to Tsu-Ming. While in graduate school in Cincinnati, he had traveled there on a field trip to study the local geological formations. Little did I know that before long Ishpeming would become familiar to me, too.

In one of his letters, Tsu-Ming expressed the desire to meet me. I wrote back, telling him that I was spending

summer vacation with my family in Washington, and he asked for my schedule and itinerary. I was taking a Greyhound bus, which was scheduled to make several stops, including one in Nashville, Tennessee. He said he would meet me there at the bus station. He drove all the way from Minneapolis in his little car, a Nash, and was waiting for me when I stepped out of the bus. I recognized him right away, of course: he was the only Chinese person waiting for the bus. My first impression was that he was a very honest and sincere person. When he found out that my next stop was Knoxville, he offered to drive me there so we could have time to get better acquainted. Because we had corresponded since January, I had developed a trust in him, and

I accepted his offer. We talked about our families and our backgrounds, and especially about growing up in China. When we got to Knoxville, Tsu-Ming saw to it that I got back on the bus and then drove home. Later, I was reimbursed by Greyhound Lines Inc. for the cost of my trip from Nashville to Knoxville, something I doubt would happen today.

The following Christmas, in 1954, I was not going home; I had been invited to the Clarks' house for the holidays. Tsu-Ming asked if he could come visit me. I said I needed to ask the Clarks. I did, and they said that any of my friends were welcome in their home. Tsu-Ming flew to Fort Worth, Texas, and then drove to El Dorado, Arkansas, where he spent a few days with me and we got to know each other even better. The next spring, after I had finished my classes and returned home, Tsu-Ming came to Washington to meet my parents. He drove by himself all the way from Ishpeming, stayed about a week helping my father paint our house, and drove back. My parents accepted him and seemed to like him.

I heard from Tsu-Ming for the first time in a letter postmarked January 23, 1954. He neglected to put my last name on the envelope, but the letter got to me anyway!

Foreground: I began my internship in medical technology at Saginaw General Hospital in Saginaw, Michigan, in July 1955. Here I am, getting ready to report for duty.

Background: When I decided to take the internship in Saginaw, I thought it would be closer to Ishpeming than Minneapolis or Chicago. What I didn't realize was that Saginaw was in Michigan's Lower Peninsula, and Ishpeming, in its Upper Peninsula. To get from one to another required taking a ferry.

Chapter 15
MY MICHIGAN INTERNSHIP

During my junior year of college, I started looking into the one-year internship I would need to complete to get my degree and become a medical technologist. I already knew that I wanted to go to the Midwest for my training in order to be closer to Tsu-Ming. I also needed to find a program at a hospital offering a student stipend. There was one in Minneapolis, one in Chicago, and one in Saginaw, Michigan. I assumed that because Saginaw was in Michigan it must be closer to Ishpeming, where Tsu-Ming was working, than Minneapolis or Chicago, so I applied there and was accepted. Actually, Saginaw, Chicago, and Minneapolis are all about the same distance from Ishpeming, but I did not know that the state of Michigan is divided into two peninsulas: Upper and Lower Michigan, separated by the Straits of Mackinac. Ishpeming is located in the Upper Peninsula, and crossing from one peninsula to the other involved taking a ferry. That meant it took longer to get to Ishpeming from Saginaw than from Minneapolis or Chicago. Later, when the Mackinac Bridge was opened in 1957, the trip took less time.

In July 1955, I began my internship at the four hundred-bed Saginaw General Hospital, earning a stipend of one hundred dollars a month. I was one of only two students in the program; the other was a girl from Bay City, Michigan. We had different instructors in each of the six departments where we worked: hematology, blood banking, bacteriology, urinalysis, histology, and blood chemistry. We had to learn to do everything manually because at that time there were no machines to help. Dr. Robert Bucklin was the director of the lab, and Joan Hall was the chief technologist. One other employee, a girl of Mexican descent, sharpened the needles that we used and then sterilized them in the autoclave. Not many items were disposable.

One requirement of the program was to observe an autopsy, something I was very glad to only do once. Another unpleasant experience that was required about three-quarters of the way through our training was spending time on call. One night when I was on call I was awakened during the night for an emergency. When I got to the lab I found

During my internship in Saginaw, I rented a small bedroom with kitchen privileges in this farmhouse. Even though this photo was taken on March 7, 1956, there was still snow on the ground.

out there had been a terrible car accident that gravely injured a young woman. She needed a transfusion as soon as possible. I went to the emergency room to draw her blood. She was lying on a stretcher and I saw that her forehead had been crushed. She was unconscious, but still breathing. I had a hard time drawing her blood because her blood pressure had dropped drastically. Then I had to do a test to determine her blood type, and I had to work quickly and accurately. When I was more than halfway through the cross matching, a call came from the emergency room and I was told to stop because she had just expired. Although I didn't know her at all I was so affected by this news that I almost cried.

While in Saginaw, I rented a small bedroom with kitchen privileges in a big farmhouse owned by a couple whose children had grown up and moved away. Most of the others renting rooms there were also connected to the hospital. One of them was a girl named Jean Falk from Petoskey, Michigan, located about one hundred and seventy miles north of Saginaw. Jean, who worked in food service at the hospital, was a few years older than I, and we became good friends. Several times she invited me to go home with her to Petoskey on the weekends. There I met her parents, who were very kind people and treated me like their own daughter. Jean's father worked as the caretaker of several cottages around Walloon Lake. The famous writer Ernest Hemingway owned one of them. A few times I went with Jean and her father to inspect the cottages, and got to see some very beautiful houses!

After working in the lab for a while, I got to know and like my coworkers quite well. One of them even took me to the Michigan State Fair. I had no idea what a state fair was, but it turned out to be a very pleasant experience. To supplement my income while working in the lab, I went to the local employment office and applied for a part-time job. I had to tell them that I could only work in the evenings or on weekends because I was in school. I got a job as a babysitter taking care of three children under the age of seven. Their mother had contracted polio and was confined in a rehabilitation center, and I was hired to watch the children when their father went to visit her. My job included getting supper for the children and putting them to bed. I had no trouble with the two older boys but the little three-year-old girl gave me a hard time. She would not go to bed! I remember that I had to walk seventeen blocks to their house. It was early evening when I went there, but late at night, and dark, when I had to walk back home.

While in Saginaw I looked for a church to attend. I found a Baptist church that was not too far from where I lived, so I started attending services there. I met an elderly lady, Mrs. Ruth Chambers, who befriended me. She was a widow with an adopted daughter, Carol, who was my age and was working in another city at the time. Like Jean's parents, Mrs. Chambers also treated me as if I were her own daughter, and I called her "Mother Chambers." She frequently invited me to her home for lunch after church, and after lunch we played Scrabble. In fact, she was the one who taught me how to play the game, which I came to enjoy very much. Later, I met Carol and we became good

One of the friends I made in Saginaw was Jean Falk, who worked in food service at Saginaw General. Here we are on a weekend trip to Walloon Lake, where her father worked.

friends. In fact, I asked her to be one of my bridesmaids when Tsu-Ming and I were married.

Several times during the year of my training at Saginaw General, Tsu-Ming drove down from Ishpeming, where he was boarding at the home of Erwin and Dorothy Johns, to visit me for the weekend. Erwin and Dorothy treated him like their own son, who at the time was serving in the military and stationed in Germany. Once when Tsu-Ming came to visit, he took me to see Lake Superior. Another time, we visited a farm where red beets were being harvested. On other weekends, he took me to Ishpeming, where I stayed in a room at the Johns' home, and to Chicago to visit a Chinese family he had met in Negaunee in the Upper Peninsula. These were very interesting and enjoyable experiences for me. On one of his trips to Saginaw, Tsu-Ming proposed to me and I accepted. He contacted my parents to let them know, and presented me with a diamond engagement ring. We set a date for our wedding: July 21, 1956.

Opposite top: Tsu-Ming boarded in Ishpeming with Erwin and Dorothy Johns. Here he is, with his first car—a Nash—in front of their home.

Opposite bottom: Here I am with Tsu-Ming's Nash. We made several trips together in this car during the year I spent in Saginaw.

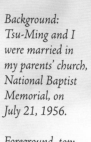

Background:
Tsu-Ming and I
were married in
my parents' church,
National Baptist
Memorial, on
July 21, 1956.

Foreground, top:
Tsu-Ming and
I pose for our
wedding photo.

Foreground,
bottom: Our
marriage
certificate, signed
by my father,
who officiated.

No. 404404   **CERTIFICATE OF MARRIAGE**

I hereby certify that on this 21st day of July,
1956, at National Baptist Memorial Church, Tsu-Ming Han
and Joy Mei-Ju Lee were by me united in marriage,
in accordance with the license issued by the Clerk of the United States
District Court for the District of Columbia.

Name Rev. Peter H. H. Lee

Residence 3310 - 19th St. N.W.
Washington 10, D.C.

To be delivered to contracting parties.

Chapter 16

NIAGARA FALLS, THE NORTHERN LIGHTS, AND NEWLYWED LIFE

At the end of June 1956, after finishing my internship, I got my degree—a BS in biology—and my certification in medical technology, which I felt was quite an accomplishment. I then went back to Washington to prepare for our wedding. The night before, we held a rehearsal at my parents' church, National Baptist Memorial Church, on Sixteenth Street at Columbia Road. During the rehearsal, my brother Samuel, who was the best man, suddenly said, "The ring!" That was when it dawned on Tsu-Ming that he had put my wedding ring in the safety deposit box of his bank in Ishpeming and had forgotten to get it out before he left for Washington. The next day, the morning of our wedding, we went to a jewelry store and Tsu-Ming bought me another ring, a platinum band. So, I got two wedding rings! My father officiated at the wedding, along with one of the church's assistant pastors. The reception immediately following our wedding was very simple: no dinner, only wedding cake and cookies. After going

home and changing clothes, Tsu-Ming and I went on our way to the Upper Peninsula of Michigan.

The first night, we reached Atlantic City, New Jersey, and the next morning enjoyed walking on its famous boardwalk along the Atlantic Ocean. We then drove to New York City and toured the Empire State Building, the tallest building in the United States at the time. That night we went to Rockefeller Center and saw a musical performance by the Rockettes. We traveled through upstate New York, visiting Albany, touring the Finger Lakes region, and taking a boat ride on an underground river in Howe Caverns. We crossed into Canada from Buffalo, New York, and drove to Niagara Falls, where we enjoyed the night view. The next morning, we walked along the path through the beautiful Oakes Garden Theatre across from the falls, and later that day we drove through Ontario, Canada, to Sudbury, where we stayed the night. Sudbury was a desolate place because the nickel mines in

尼加拉瀑布，北極光和新婚生活

Top: My entire family gathered for this wedding photo. Left to right: Joseph, Samuel, Lois, my mother, me, Tsu-Ming, my father, Eugene, and James.

Bottom left: One of the stops we made on our honeymoon trip was at Niagara Falls. Here I am standing under Bridal Veil Falls.

Bottom right: This photo was taken of me, still a new bride, shortly after we arrived in Ishpeming.

In Ishpeming, Erwin and Dorothy Johns hosted a reception for me and Tsu-Ming. Here we are, with Dorothy Johns on the right.

that region had done great harm to the vegetation. Only stumps remained of the trees that had once stood there. On the sixth day of our trip, just before arriving in Ishpeming, I remember seeing a display of the northern lights.

By now, Tsu-Ming had been working at Cleveland-Cliffs for four years, all the while boarding with Erwin and Dorothy Johns for eight dollars a week. Shortly before we were married, he rented an upstairs apartment in a house owned by a very kind, childless couple, Arne and Borghild Nelson, on North Pine Street. It became our first home. The Johns had helped Tsu-Ming select furniture and

other household items for the apartment, and his colleagues at the iron company had given him a number of gifts. I had received many gifts at wedding showers in Washington and Saginaw, and after we arrived in Ishpeming, Tsu-Ming's church gave me another shower, at which we received still more gifts! So, we were well equipped to set up housekeeping immediately. It took me several months just to write thank-you notes!

Looking back, I cannot say our marriage was always the happiest. Tsu-Ming was a rather mild-mannered person, while I consider myself more strong willed. He was also more patient than I. Yet he never

Tsu-Ming took this photo of me on December 25, 1956, my first Christmas in Ishpeming. I felt like I was on an Arctic expedition!

looked down on me, and I believe he considered me his equal. Over the years we did have differences of opinions on certain things, but we never shouted at each other. I think we made a good team.

Once we settled down, I enjoyed some leisure time. I was welcomed into the Ishpeming Newcomers Club, and started taking driver's training, which was offered at the local high school. We were faced with one frightening experience at that time: Tsu-Ming was summoned to the courthouse in Marquette, Michigan, and questioned by the FBI. It was in connection with a meeting he had attended before we were married of a University

of Minnesota Chinese student organization that, unbeknownst to Tsu-Ming, had Communist leanings. This came just at the end of the McCarthy era, during which thousands of Americans were accused of being Communist sympathizers. Several people from Cleveland-Cliffs testified on Tsu-Ming's behalf and, much to our relief, nothing ever came of it.

After a while, I began looking for a job and found one as a medical technician at St. Mary's, a Catholic hospital in Marquette, Michigan, about fifteen miles northeast of Ishpeming on the shore of Lake Superior. I remember interviewing for the job, presenting my credentials, and being hired on the spot. The lab was very small, staffed by only one technician who was leaving to take another job. I started working immediately.

My shift began at seven o'clock in the morning, but because we had only one car, Tsu-Ming had to get me there even earlier so he could get back to Cleveland-Cliffs by seven, when he also had to start work. The director of the hospital was Mother Adolgonda, a nun who was feared by the employees. Happily, I did not have much contact with her. The chief physician at the hospital was Dr. Wilbur Casler, an older doctor whom I actually had met, through Tsu-Ming, not long after coming to Ishpeming and before I was hired to work at St. Mary's. Some years earlier, Dr. Casler and his wife, Florence, had invited Tsu-Ming to their home to meet a Chinese girl who was staying with them while she attended Northern Michigan University. At least twice while I was working at St. Mary's the Caslers housed me overnight on winter evenings when Tsu-Ming could not pick me up because of heavy snowfalls. One time he did try, but didn't get very far. The car slid into a snowbank and got stuck. He had to walk to a gas station and call a colleague at the

research lab, who came with a truck and pulled him out.

Meanwhile, Tsu-Ming's work was going well. Over the years, his research findings, which he published and presented at various scientific meetings, described how iron ore deposits formed geologically. His work also led to improvements in the process of concentrating raw iron ore into higher-grade iron ore pellets used for making steel. The pellets had to be both free of contaminating materials and crush resistant for transport to distant steel mills.

Tsu-Ming's work at the Cleveland-Cliffs Iron Company led to improvements in the way raw iron was turned into high-quality iron ore pellets for the steel industry.

Chapter 17
CHILDREN OF OUR OWN

I worked at St. Mary's, enjoying my job very much, for about eight months, until the spring of 1957. Then I decided to stop working to await the birth of our first baby, due in mid-June.

In early May, I went with Tsu-Ming to attend a meeting on the campus of Michigan State University in East Lansing, Michigan. Back home in Ishpeming, in the early morning hours of May 22, I started hemorrhaging. Tsu-Ming called my physician, Archie Narotzky, but was told he was unavailable and that one of his colleagues, Dr. Louis Rosenbaum, would visit me at home. After examining me, he determined that I had a condition called placenta previa and said I should go to the hospital immediately. Shortly after Tsu-Ming and I arrived, Dr. Narotzky performed an emergency cesarean section, and our first son was born. Although it did not matter to me whether our firstborn child was a boy or a girl, I knew that Tsu-Ming wished for a boy, even though he had never said so. With the help of "Grandma" Dorothy Johns, we decided to name him Dennis, a name we liked and which at the time was

not too common. We also liked the singer Dennis Day, who was popular then.

The night before Dennis was born we had been visiting our close friends, Ted and Joyce Engel, who had a young son. Joyce's second baby was also due at that time. I beat her to it, but not by much! Three days later, a lady was admitted to my hospital room, and to my surprise, it was Joyce! She had had a baby girl. But even though her baby was born after mine, she was discharged before me. At that time, C-section patients had to stay in the hospital at least a week. I was there for nine days.

When I returned home, I was very weak and needed a lot of help with the housework and cooking. Tsu-Ming had to take on more responsibilities at home in addition to going to work. It was hard at first. Borghild, who was still our landlady, had a sister who was a registered nurse and worked as the nurse at the local school. Her name was Thelma Steve. Her husband was named Con, short for Conrad, and he worked as a carpenter at Cleveland-Cliffs. They had no children. Thelma came to visit frequently and

我們自己的孩子

Opposite foreground: Dennis, our first-born son, was born on May 22, 1957.

Opposite background: Tsu-Ming and I became US citizens in 1961 and 1962, respectively.

helped me a great deal. She and Borghild became very close to Dennis. They truly adored him. Later on, Con made a play-pen for Dennis. They invited us to their house for supper a few times and we became lifelong friends.

Our second son, Timothy Mark, was born in April, 1958. His initials, T.M., were the same as Tsu-Ming's. At the time, a couple who lived just north of us gave us the most wonderful gift: their old baby buggy. This buggy was unique in that it had four wheels and a pair of steel runners. Both the wheels and the runners could be raised or lowered. In summer, I used the

Dennis was nine months old when Tsu-Ming took this photo of us in front of a giant pile of snow.

Bottom: Our second son, Tim, was born on April 7, 1958, and ten days old when he and I left St. Mary's Hospital.

wheels, and in winter, the runners. I would put both boys in the buggy and go visit Thelma and Con, who by then were both retired. I truly enjoyed those visits.

In 1960, when the boys were three and two years old, we were offered a company house to rent on North Street, two blocks east of Lake Bancroft—a small lake one could walk around in less than an hour—and two blocks from a playground. We had been pretty crowded in our three-room apartment, so we took it gladly. The one and-a-half-story house had been built years earlier for a very important person in the company and his family, and it had hardwood floors and built-in drawers and cabinets throughout. The front yard was surrounded by a low, white, picket fence. The front door of the house opened onto an enclosed porch with big windows on three sides. The main floor consisted of a living room, two bedrooms, and a kitchen big enough to include a dining area. The upstairs was set up as one big dormitory-like room with a small, full bathroom that included a claw-foot bathtub. I will never forget how at first, both Dennis and Tim were afraid of the tub, and didn't want to get in. Thankfully, that didn't last long. The house also had a full basement.

The rent was only fifty dollars a month and Cleveland-Cliffs workers took care of

washing all the outside windows. In the winter, they also put on the storm windows, and in the spring, they took them down. Suddenly we had it good! We were very grateful, and lived in the house for ten years. The only drawback: the backyard was very narrow, and dropped straight down to the neighbor's backyard. The children were forbidden to go back there, and instead spent a lot of time at the nearby playground, which had a viewing stand for basketball, tennis, and other sports, and a running track. They loved it there.

About the same time that we moved into the house on North Street, I found

One of the best presents we ever received was a baby buggy equipped with both wheels and steel runners. Thanks to the runners, I was able to get out and about during the long Upper Peninsula winters with Dennis (left) and Tim (right).

Dennis (left) and Tim (right) were born less than a year apart, and kept me very busy.

part-time work as a medical technologist at our local hospital, Francis A. Bell Memorial, working Monday through Friday mornings. An older woman named Alice Racine took care of Dennis and Tim, who came to think of her like their grandma. During the summer, I walked a half hour to and from work, starting out at six thirty in the morning. In winter, when it was too cold or slippery, Tsu-Ming would drive me to the hospital. I really enjoyed my work and made quite a few friends among my coworkers and a few of the hospital's nurses.

In 1962, we experienced both sadness and joy. On April 6, our daughter was born, bringing us great happiness. We named her Lisa Ruth, after my mother. But later that month, my paternal grandmother died in Shanghai at the age of ninety-five. She had been a very important part of my life, and I was devastated at the thought of never seeing her again. On December 4, I achieved another goal: I was granted my US citizenship, something Tsu-Ming had achieved one year earlier. I remember going to the

courthouse in Marquette, Michigan, putting my hand on a Bible, and swearing my allegiance to the United States. I had studied very hard to pass the written citizenship test, and the ceremony was very meaningful to me. By then, I really felt like an American, especially when it came to my lifestyle and values. I still loved and was proud of my Chinese culture, which is part of who I am, but it wasn't difficult to give up my Chinese citizenship.

Nai-Nai, my paternal grandmother, died at the age of ninety-five in 1962. My relatives in China sent me this photograph taken at her grave in Shanghai.

Foreground: By the fall of 1962 when this photo was taken, I was the mother of three children (left to right: Dennis, Lisa, and Tim) under the age of five.

Background: We built our house on Duncan Avenue in 1968 on land we bought from Cleveland-Cliffs Iron Company.

Chapter 18

A JOB, FAMILY LIFE, AND CHINESE DUMPLINGS

I took a leave of absence from Bell Memorial for one and a half years when Lisa was a baby, and then went back to my job. I wanted to put my education to use, and I enjoyed working as a medical technologist. I also wanted to keep up with new developments in the field. I stayed on part time at the hospital until my retirement in 1994.

As the children grew older they wanted their own bedrooms, and in 1968 we built a new house on a sloped lot on Duncan Avenue. The property, which was very close to the Al Quaal Recreation Area north of Ishpeming, had been owned by Cleveland-Cliffs. We settled on a bi-level house with the main floor facing the street and the back door on the lower level. The house had three bedrooms, a study, and two fireplaces. We added a deck on the back of the house and eventually finished the lower level by adding a family room, two more bedrooms, a bathroom, and a laundry room. This is the place where my children grew up and where I still live.

I was quite busy, at first raising two boys very close in age, and before long, three children under five, and the bitterly cold Upper Peninsula winters were particularly challenging. I didn't really like winter, but I had to get used to it. Often the snow was up over the windows on the first floor, and during a terrible blizzard in March 1979 we had so much snow that when I opened the garage door I could see only the roof of my neighbor's house across the street. Everyone helped shovel snow and sometimes we had to dig tunnels to get out of the house. In Ishpeming, they cleared the roads almost right away and you could hear the plows at two or three o'clock in the morning. And the Ishpeming Public Schools never closed unless there was an especially severe blizzard. The kids loved winter. We have home movies of them jumping into huge snow piles and crawling through a snow tunnel to get to the sidewalk.

From grade school through high school, the children participated in lots of

工作，家居生活和餃子

This was the view from inside our garage on March 8, 1979.

a wood carver and made his own toys and games, some of which I still have.

When I wasn't busy with the children I loved to read, knit, and crochet. I tried sewing, but even though my grandmother had been a seamstress, I found I didn't like it. However, my sister, Lois, took up sewing and made many beautiful, useful things. Tsu-Ming enjoyed following the Detroit Tigers and Green Bay Packers, bowling in a local league, and taking an occasional fishing trip. He loved taking photographs and movies, and he always had his camera nearby. Tsu-Ming also liked to cook, and one of his specialties was Chinese dumplings. However, one day while cooking he started thinking about his work at the lab and walked away from the stove. I came home to find the whole house filled with smoke. We were lucky it didn't burn down. He was like an absent-minded professor.

Over the years we took several family trips, including one to Jackson Hole, Wyoming. We were also active in the churches we attended, first the Bible Baptist Church, not far from where we used to live, and later, Calvary Baptist Church in Negaunee.

Tsu-Ming and I instilled in our children the value of education, which was very important to us. For example, we insisted that they do their homework

activities sponsored by our local school district and others nearby: tennis, table tennis, volleyball, skiing, skating, and tobogganing. One winter when Dennis was in junior high school he wanted to sign up for skiing in the UP Community School Winter Games, but the slots were filled. Instead, he decided to take figure skating. Tsu-Ming and I took him to Negaunee, about three miles away, where there was a rink. He fell down again and again, but he kept at it until there was an opening in another sport. Lisa loved animals, and over the years we had a number of pets: a dog, goldfish, and gerbils. Tim was the most creative of the three children. He was

Tsu-Ming occasionally went ice fishing. Here he is out on the ice in 1999.

before they could play with their friends. When they were in grade school, we (mostly just me, because Tsu-Ming was working) never missed parent/teacher conferences. Their teachers always said that they were good pupils and very well behaved. I was very happy to hear that. Dennis, Tim, and Lisa all turned out to be smart, and graduated with high honors from Ishpeming High School. Dennis and Lisa were co-valedictorians, and Tim placed in the top one percent of his class. Dennis really liked school, but when people would comment on how smart he was, he would say, "No, I just know how to study." All were involved in sports and music. Dennis and Tim played on the tennis team, and Lisa participated in downhill skiing, basketball, and track. All three were in school bands. I remember following their teams and attending their concerts. I wanted to be involved with all their activities to show that I was interested in what they did. They loved it when I showed up.

I don't remember ever sitting Dennis, Tim, and Lisa down and teaching them about Chinese values or ethics, although we did talk about the importance of filial piety, the Confucian philosophy that stresses respect for one's parents, elders, and ancestors. I also assumed the

Even though my Chinese culture was important to me, one of my wishes was for Dennis, Lisa, and Tim to grow up as normal, American children.

our children were obedient and rarely gave us any trouble. Still, as they got older and developed minds of their own and were influenced more by their friends, it became harder to discipline them. I remember one really severe winter evening when Dennis was a young teenager and wanted to go to a movie with some of his friends in Marquette, fifteen miles away. One of the older boys was going to drive, but I said, "No, you are not going." He said, "My friends' parents are letting them go. Why won't you let me?" I said, "I don't care what their parents do. I am your parent and you are not going." He was very mad at me and pouted the rest of the night and even the next day.

children would observe the way we lived our daily lives. For example, we lived frugally. I remember we had the same washer and dryer for fifty years. In fact, the kids thought we were poor because we never had flashy things. But we never went into debt. We never had a mortgage, and never used credit cards. We paid as we went. I think that was an example of our Chinese values. I did try to teach our children Chinese before they went to school. They learned a little bit, but it was hard.

Looking back, I guess we were strict—Chinese parents seem to be more strict than American parents—but in general,

When the children were growing up, we were the only Chinese family in town, and even today only 0.3 percent of Ishpeming's population is Asian. Of course, living in Ishpeming, I felt isolated from my culture. To compensate, I often cooked traditional Chinese meals, even though we had to travel to Chicago or Milwaukee to find some of the ingredients I needed. But I missed speaking Chinese and having friends whose backgrounds were similar to mine and with whom I could celebrate the Chinese New Year and the Autumn Moon Festival. These holidays had been a big part of my childhood and

I wished I had friends in Ishpeming who could understand how I felt about their importance.

On the other hand, I can honestly say that I personally never experienced any prejudice in America. From the time I arrived in the United States as a young woman, through my college years, and for all the years I lived in Ishpeming, I felt accepted for who I was. Many years ago, Tsu-Ming did receive some threats, mostly in the form of anonymous phone calls. I don't know if the threats came about solely because we were Chinese, or if some people who didn't know us resented the fact that Tsu-Ming had a well-paying job at Cleveland-Cliffs' research lab. For a while, he kept a shotgun, which the children were sternly warned not to touch, in the back of his closet. I think this was because Tsu-Ming had grown up in a family living under the constant threat of violence and in a household that had been armed. Much later, when our children were older, we found out that some of their classmates had made fun of them for being different.

They didn't want to tell us because they were afraid we would be upset. Instead, they just ignored the teasing. What else could they do?

Still, overall, Ishpeming turned out to be a good place to raise my family and pursue my career, and I feel that, for the most part, being Chinese was not an issue for our family. Nevertheless, I will never forget the kindness of the Nelsons and the Johns, who welcomed us, a young Chinese couple, to town in 1956, and our many other good friends. I think that we were well respected, largely because of Tsu-Ming's work and research, which helped bring jobs to the area by expanding the local mining industry to include the nearby Empire and Tilden Mines. And because our children did very well in school, they earned the admiration of their teachers. They also had good friends, which for me was very important. Lastly, even though my culture was a big part of my life, I wanted Dennis, Tim, and Lisa to grow up as normal American children. And in Ishpeming, they did.

Chapter 19
THE UNIVERSITY OF MICHIGAN

Of course, Tsu-Ming and I also wanted our children to become well educated, a wish they fulfilled. By the time he was in high school, Dennis was interested in medicine and had decided to pursue it. At that time, the University of Michigan, in Ann Arbor, offered a six-year, integrated premedical–medical school program known as Inteflex. Only fifty students a year out of hundreds who applied were accepted into the program. I remember Dennis had to fill out a long application that looked like a book with many, many pages, including some essay questions. He sent it in and then had to wait. Meanwhile, a neighbor who had also graduated from Michigan interviewed Dennis and recommended him.

Dennis also applied to Harvard University, and was recommended for admission by Herman Gundlach, a Harvard alum who ran a big construction company in Houghton, Michigan. In the end, Dennis was accepted to both Michigan and Harvard. After deciding to accept Michigan's offer, someone from Harvard called our home to ask Dennis why he had turned them down. Dennis told them it was because of Michigan's six-year program. I thought that was a good reason. I was happy he chose the University of Michigan because I didn't want him going far away. After medical school, Dennis specialized in ophthalmology and accepted an academic position at the Medical College of Wisconsin Eye Institute, in Milwaukee, where he practiced retinal surgery and became a professor. While in medical school, Dennis met Mary Lynn Musial, a student in the School of Nursing. They were married in 1982 and have two sons.

Tim had been interested in dentistry ever since he was a little boy, intrigued mostly by the instruments the dentist used on his teeth. Following Dennis's example, he also applied to the University of Michigan. But when he applied only there, I became worried, and asked him, "What if you are not accepted?" But he was. And, after only two years of undergraduate work, he took and passed the entrance exam for the university's School of Dentistry. In the summers Tim also followed in Dennis's footsteps by working in the iron mines. Following graduation,

密歇根大學

Opposite: By 1980 when this photo was taken, Lisa, Dennis, and Tim were all in college.

Dennis graduated from the University of Michigan's six-year, premedical-medical program in 1981.

back to Ishpeming, we both began crying. We cried some more when we got home and saw her empty bedroom. After graduating, Lisa attended the Columbia Graduate School of Bible and Missions in Columbia, South Carolina. Then she attended graduate school at the University of Wisconsin–Madison, where she met her future husband, Quinn Ellner, a medical technologist. They were married on my birthday, October 29, in 1988. Lisa and Quinn have three children: a boy, and a set of twins—a boy and a girl. In 1999, when their children were three and six years old, Lisa and Quinn moved the family to China to teach English. Tsu-Ming was against the move, mostly because it was so far away. Of course, I missed them a lot, but believed that if it was God's will, they should go. I've been to China to visit them five times, at first with Tsu-Ming and then by myself or with Dennis and his boys.

he worked as a dentist in the Lake George region of upstate New York, where he met his future wife, Cindy North. Later, Tim joined the US Air Force and served as an Air Force dentist at Bolling Air Force Base in Washington, DC. After that, he practiced dentistry in North Carolina for several years before enrolling at the Medical University of South Carolina, in Charleston, where he received his MD. He then practiced medicine in Wilmington, North Carolina.

Lisa went to the University of Michigan as well, and majored in wildlife management in the School of Natural Resources. I remember that after Tsu-Ming and I dropped her off in Ann Arbor for her freshman year and started driving

Meanwhile, all of my siblings had also become very well educated. After graduating from Carson-Newman College in Jefferson City, Tennessee, Lois went to medical school at Wake Forest School of Medicine in Winston-Salem, North Carolina. She became an anesthesiologist and for a while worked at Doctors Hospital in Washington, DC. After her marriage to Henry Lin, an engineer who started his own company, they moved to Ocala, Florida. After Samuel earned his MD at Vanderbilt, he completed his internship and residency in pathology at Baltimore's Johns Hopkins Hospital, and in 1966 was appointed assistant chief of pathology at the US Public Health Service Hospital.

Joseph attended the LeTourneau Institute of Technology in Longview, Texas, before transferring to Texas A&M, where during his junior year he enlisted in the US Air Force. The Air Force sent him to Oklahoma State University to complete his bachelor's degree in aerospace engineering. It was there that he met, and later married, Cathy Chung. After resigning from the service, he returned to Texas A&M to get a master's degree. Eventually he took a job in research and development at the US Army's Aberdeen, Maryland, Proving Ground, working on the army's helicopter systems. He retired twenty-one years ago and now lives in Bel Air, Maryland.

My two youngest brothers attended the University of Maryland in College Park. Eugene studied computer science—he was a whiz with computers, even back then—and worked in Washington, DC. He remained single, and is now retired and living in Greenbelt, Maryland. James went into social work, specializing in

children and family services. He worked his entire career for the State of Maryland. He married a Chinese woman from Taiwan named Pauline Wu who opened her own Chinese restaurant in Gaithersburg, Maryland. Later, they moved to Las Vegas to be close to their only daughter, Rebecca, who was living there after her marriage.

Top: Lisa married Quinn Ellner on my birthday, October 29, in 1988. Left to right: Me, Tim, Lisa, Quinn, Dennis, and Tsu-Ming.

Bottom: Lisa and Quinn moved to China in 1999 to teach English. Here they are with their three children in July 2000.

Chapter 20
CHINA: THIRTY YEARS LATER

In 1979, after thirty years of Communist control of China, the government opened the country's doors to the West. For those thirty years, we had had no news of our family or friends in China, and so my parents decided to go back in September to search for our long-lost relatives. When Joseph and I learned of their plans, we decided to join them, believing it might be their last trip to China, and that reconnecting with our aunts and cousins would be much easier with their help.

I took a two-month leave of absence from my job at Bell Memorial, renewed my passport, applied for a visa, and bought the round-trip ticket for my trip. My parents, brother, and I flew from different cities to meet in Chicago. Because there were no direct flights to mainland China, we had to fly a roundabout way: first to Alaska, then to Tokyo and Taiwan, and finally, to Hong Kong!

In Hong Kong, my parents' friends, Mr. and Mrs. Deng, arranged for us to stay in the Astor Hotel, where they had reserved rooms for us. We were deathly tired after our long, arduous journey, and after

registering at the front desk, we went into our rooms and immediately fell into bed, totally exhausted! Later, the Dengs brought us our supper but had to wait in the lobby until we woke up.

We stayed in Hong Kong about a week, going to a bank to exchange travelers' checks into Chinese currency and to a tourist office to arrange our trip into mainland China, and buying gifts for friends and relatives. Hong Kong, which at the time was still under British control, had changed a lot since I had been there in 1950 on my way to the United States. There were more high-rise buildings and many more people than I remembered. While we were in Hong Kong, the Dengs took us to a Chinese restaurant. The method of ordering food there was unique. We were seated at a table and servers came to us, pushing carts displaying many different dishes on three levels. We pointed to what we wanted and the food was put on our table.

We knew that most Bibles had been destroyed during the Chinese Cultural Revolution, the decade beginning in 1966 when China's political leaders attempted

祖國：三十年後

Opposite foreground: By the time the Cultural Revolution ended in 1976, Chinese Christians were desperately seeking out God's word. I could see this for myself when I visited Shanghai's very crowded Grace Church in 1979.

Opposite background: The Terracotta Army, a collection of thousands of life-sized sculptures that had been buried in the tomb of China's first emperor, was discovered in 1974.

113

to strengthen the government's Communist ideology partly by attacking traditional Chinese values, and that many Christians were desperately wishing for God's Word. So we went to a Christian publishing house and purchased one hundred Chinese Bibles. We also bought copies of a devotional book, *Streams in the Desert*, by Lettie Cowman, which Chinese Christians treasured most, after the Bible.

We knew we would have to smuggle the books into China, which would not be easy because our belongings would be thoroughly searched at the border crossing. Still, we had to try. The most the authorities could do was confiscate them; because we were US citizens with valid US passports they would not be able to prosecute

or imprison us. We decided to divide the books and carry them spread out in the bottom of our luggage under our clothing. We took a short train ride from Kowloon, in Hong Kong, to Guangzhou, the first city on the southern border of mainland China, where we had to go through immigration checks in one of two tents: one for men and one for women. It was a slow process that included body searches. At the inspection building we all lined up in a big hall with long tables on each side. Those arriving had to go through the middle of the hall, placing their luggage on the tables in front of the inspectors.

We were at the end of the line because our luggage had not arrived with us from the train. Our parents went ahead with

On our trip to China in 1979, my parents, brother, and I smuggled in one hundred Chinese Bibles.

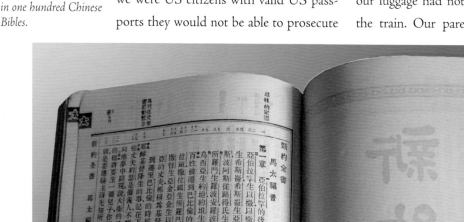

their small carry-on bags while Joseph and I waited for our large suitcases at the entrance to the hall. By the time they were finally delivered, the hall was crowded with people having their luggage searched or waiting in line for their turn. My brother and I each pulled two suitcases into the hall. Noticing that the inspectors were busy searching other luggage, Joseph whispered to me: "Let's just walk through. Don't stop." We walked all the way to the other end of the hall where our parents were waiting for us. No one stopped us, reminding me of the time I had snuck into Hong Kong in 1950.

In Guangzhou we stayed several days in the Overseas Chinese Friendship Hotel, a hotel especially for Chinese returning from a foreign country. The China Travel Service had arranged our inland itinerary, and while in Guangzhou we did some sightseeing, viewing a cultural exhibit and walking along the bank of the Pearl River, one of the three main rivers in China. (The other two are the Yellow River in the north and the Yangtze River in central China.) I also walked back and forth across the bridge over the Pearl River, which had separate lanes for cars, bicycles, and pedestrians.

Our main purpose in going to China was to look up the relatives and friends we had lost contact with between 1949 and 1979, when China had been closed to the rest of the world. And so from Guangzhou we took the train to Zhengzhou, the provincial capital of Henan Province and the city to which many of my relatives had moved. It was the longest train ride I had ever experienced, taking more than two days! There, we were on our own because there was no travel service to take care of us. We got a taxi to take us to a hotel and tried to find out where our relatives were living. While we were checking in, a man I did not recognize came up to us, introduced himself as the hotel manager, and said that he had heard we were coming. He had reserved rooms for us, had arranged a private minibus with a driver to take us anywhere we needed to go, and had contacted my cousin Cheng Xiufang to let

The train ride I took from Guangzhou to Zhengzhou took more than two days. Left to right: Joseph, my father, my mother, and me.

Top: In Zhengzhou, I was reunited with my cousin Cheng Xiufang (to my left, in white) and her family. Xiufang's husband is at the far left of photo.

Bottom: In Zhengzhou, I also was reunited with my high school principal, Wu Huimin (seated, third from left).

her know we would be in Zhengzhou. We were so relieved and thankful! It turned out that he had been a classmate of mine at Sacred Virtue School.

The next day, Xiufang and her son came to our hotel. When she saw us, she was overcome by emotion, kneeled down in front of my parents, put her head on their knees, and wept. Soon, we were all crying together. While in Zhengzhou, we went by minibus to Xiufang's home and then to a big welcoming feast she had arranged for us in a hotel dining room, where we met our younger relatives for the first time. We also met with one of my father's sisters and her family, and visited with other friends. Another highlight of our trip to Zhengzhou was reuniting with Principal Wu, who I learned had been imprisoned by the Communists for twenty-seven years as punishment for his service as an officer in the Chinese Nationalist army and for being a Christian.

After a few days, we went to Kaifeng to visit Xiufang's older sister, Xiuzheng, and her family, and the family of their sister, Xiulian, who had passed away a few years earlier. More feasts awaited us. We ate so much that I felt I would never be able to eat another meal! Again, it was a happy and noisy reunion! While in Kaifeng we also went to see the ancient Dragon Pavilion and the Iron Pagoda that I remembered climbing with my parents when I was a little girl. This time, climbing with Joseph, I made it all the way to the top. Another trip we made while we were in the area was to the Longmen Grottoes near Luoyang, where more than a thousand years ago tens of thousands of Buddhas were carved out of cliffs overlooking the Yi River.

In Kaifeng, we attended another family reunion, this one with the family of my cousin Xiuzheng (front row, far right).

After leaving Kaifeng, my parents, brother, and I visited the Longmen Grottoes in Luoyang. In this photo, my mother and I are walking in front of two of the thousands of Buddhas that were carved into stone cliffs centuries ago.

Our next stop was Xi'an, where we took a tour and saw the Terracotta Army, a collection of thousands of sculptures depicting the armies of China's first emperor, Qin Shi Huang Di, and which had been buried with him. The life-sized sculptures were discovered in 1974 and when we visited were still being excavated. While in Xi'an, I also saw Gao Yurui, who had been my best friend growing up in Kaifeng. I learned that her husband had passed away, leaving her to raise four children on her own. Still a teacher, she was living in a classroom on the second floor of her school because the teacher's dormitory was under construction. I remember

In Xi'an, I saw my dear friend Yurui (fifth from left) for the first time since my family moved out of the Baptist Compound in 1941 following the Japanese attack on Pearl Harbor. I learned that her life under Communist rule had been difficult.

meeting her there, sitting around a small table eating meals and catching up. I learned that her life under the Communist regime had been very hard.

We ended our trip with stops in Beijing and Shanghai. In Beijing, we again stayed in a hotel specifically for returning Chinese, and were invited to attend a welcoming banquet commemorating the thirtieth anniversary of the founding of the People's Republic of China and held in the Great Hall of the People. In a big room full of round tables, each seating eight people, we heard speeches and were served several courses of fabulous food. While in Beijing, we also went

sightseeing, visiting the Forbidden City, the Ming Tombs, the Summer Palace, and Beihai Park, with its famous Nine-Dragon Wall. One day when our parents went on a tour, Joseph and I decided to return to the Forbidden City. It is so vast that one cannot see it in a single day. We also booked a tour for the Great Wall, about fifty miles north of Beijing. For me, seeing and walking on the Great Wall was the highlight of our time there.

In Shanghai, we took steps to obtain the remains of my paternal grandmother —which had been dug up from her original burial site—in case the site, like many others during the Cultural Revolution, was desecrated in a misguided attempt by Red Guards to undermine traditional Chinese values and customs. They were in the care of our family friend Mr. Wu, the same man who had watched out for me, Lois, and Samuel when we first arrived in Shanghai. He continued to look after Nai-Nai after we all left for America, and after her death stored her remains in the upstairs of his home in a large cookie tin decorated with a floral pattern. Our desire was to have them cremated and hand carry the ashes to the United States. However, when we went to see Mr. Wu, only his mother was at home, and because she was superstitious about having human remains in the house, had

While in Shanghai, we were able to obtain the remains of my grandmother Nai-Nai that were stored in this decorative cookie tin my father is holding.

not been informed of their existence. To avoid revealing the real reason for our visit, we told her only, "We left something here and want to pick it up." We retrieved the cookie tin and drove in a taxi to the crematorium, where my father, wishing to take one last look at his mother's remains, took the tin to a private room for viewing. He returned with a look of shock and dismay on his face: He had found only cookies in the tin! I can only imagine his consternation as he dug through the cookies, finally realizing the mistake. We went back to Mr. Wu's home and with his help found the remains in a second, identical tin. The incident was not funny at the time, but later made a great story for me to share with family and friends.

I found the big cities in China much changed from when I was last there. Many big buildings and modern roads were under construction. And although people were still somewhat cautious about being seen speaking to foreigners—an aftereffect

Mr. Wu (front row, right) was a good friend of our family.

of the Cultural Revolution—they were willing to talk with us. It was wonderful to revisit the places we used to live, our family, and friends. And it was especially meaningful for my parents because it did turn out to be the last time they would visit China. Although my mother lived for almost thirty more years, my father died just six years after our trip while he and my mother were in Ocala, Florida, visiting Lois. My father had been on a preaching tour through the southern states, and was in Arizona when he first felt something was wrong. By the time they got to Ocala, where I was also visiting, he had to see a doctor, who ran some tests and diagnosed stage four, untreatable colon cancer. We were all shocked. I hadn't even known he was sick. We moved him to a specialized medical center, and all of my brothers came to see him before he died several weeks later. We held a service for my father in Ocala, where he was buried. And thanks to our persistence in Shanghai, the ashes of my grandmother, who in life had refused to come to the United States, were buried with her son.

Chapter 21
A PAIR OF CULTURAL AWAKENINGS

In 1980, Tsu-Ming made his first trip back to China, traveling to Beijing to attend a geology conference. While there he was reunited with two of his sisters, whom he had not seen in thirty-three years. But he also learned the sad news that during the Communist Revolution his father had been arrested, falsely accused of treason by way of working for the Chinese Nationalist government, and executed.

I traveled back to China eight more times over the next twenty-two years, the first in July 1988, when Tsu-Ming was traveling to a symposium in Beijing, and we decided to make it a family trip. We traveled to many places, including Shanghai, Zhengzhou, Kaifeng, and Beijing. At the time, few foreigners visited the interior of China, and even though we were Chinese, we still stood out among the crowd with our Western dress and hairstyles. The native Chinese were particularly curious about Tim, who was an amateur bodybuilder.

With the exception of our visits to relatives, our trip itinerary and guides were carefully managed by the China Travel Service, one of two government-run travel agencies authorized to work with foreigners visiting China. Our tour was specifically for Chinese living overseas. The guides seemed quite sincere, but presented everything with a positive spin. From the Chinese natives' standpoint, we were considered an extension of themselves, experiencing a homecoming. According to Dennis, he and his siblings at first thought of themselves simply as first-generation Chinese Americans on tour. That attitude was to change as we experienced heartfelt welcomes from relatives and family friends later in our visit.

We saw a marked contrast between the subsidized economy of China and the free market economy of the United States. Under the Communists, large enterprises were owned by the state, wages were the same whether one worked hard or not, and there was no danger of losing one's job for performing poorly. And so even though everyone had a job, there was no incentive to do it. This system of entitlement, known in China as the "iron rice

两種文化的覺醒

Opposite foreground: Tsu-Ming (fourth from left) at a family reunion in Luoyang, in 1980. It was the first time he had seen any of his relatives since leaving China in 1947.

Opposite background: Luoyang's Longmen Grottoes are one of the major tourist attractions in central China.

Tsu-Ming and I took our children to China for the first time in 1988. Here we are at the Great Wall near Beijing.

bowl," became apparent to us in a number of odd ways. For example, department store attendants both outnumbered and ignored customers. Hotels had a sleep-in attendant on every floor, but when we asked for fresh towels, we would receive damp and smelly ones. At one hotel where the receptionists were exceptionally friendly, Dennis noticed a sign promoting its "smiling to improve service campaign." Yet, we also found a robust sidewalk market economy where vendors and customers were fully engaged. The children learned from Tsu-Ming how to haggle. He told them he wouldn't stop

bargaining until a merchant got out a calculator to see if he was profiting or not.

Highlights of this trip included unusual and beautiful sights, including the mountains near Guilin, the Forbidden City, the Temple of Heaven, the Longmen Grottoes, and the Great Wall near Beijing. But their most meaningful experience, our children told us, was meeting many relatives for the first time, and some, the last. Dennis recalled, "They included a very pretty girl cousin who died within several years after our visit for lack of a kidney transplant, and my paternal grandmother, who died in 1998 at the age of 102. We also saw my dad's brother and two sisters and their families, and three of my mother's cousins and their families. We were greatly saddened to see our father grieve deeply at his first visit to my grandfather's grave, forty-one years after last seeing him alive in Shanghai as my dad departed for the United States." Dennis describes the trip as "not just an adventure, but for us, a cultural awakening and family gathering of historic proportions. For my parents, my dad in particular, it was also an experience filled with emotions of regret, joy, and great sorrow. By the end of the trip, we kids appreciated even more our good fortune in being raised in the United States."

If that trip was, indeed, a "cultural awakening" for our children, my next visit to China three years later was an awakening of a different sort for me, one that showed how different I had become from one of my peers who remained in China while I grew to adulthood in the United States. I went to see Eula, the Kaifeng schoolmate who had been my roommate when I was hospitalized in Shanghai. After I emigrated to the United States, she and I had corresponded by mail, and in 1991 she invited me to visit her, promising to take me to the Yellow Mountains in Anhui Province, which were known for their beautiful scenery. I was eager to

visit China again, and thought, "Why not accept her invitation?" The trip, however, was not as I expected. When I arrived I discovered that, much to my dismay, she had become a proud member of the Communist Party and occupied a high position in the government.

I stayed in China with Eula for three weeks, but soon got bored and frustrated. Despite her earlier promises, we never went to the Yellow Mountains. Eula said it was too dangerous, which was untrue. It is a popular site, well traveled, and not considered hazardous. (Some years later, I visited the Yellow Mountains with Tsu-Ming, and saw the *yun hai*, or "cloud sea." It is a most unusual sight that occurs when the sun comes out after a rain and the mist rising from the valley covers everything but the highest mountain peaks, making them look like islands floating in the ocean. We stayed in a beautiful hotel near the summit of the mountain for three days.) Eula did take me to visit my cousin Xiufang in Zhengzhou, which involved a train trip of more than eight hours. After the visit, my cousin called Eula *gu guai*, which roughly translated, means "odd and unpleasant."

While we were in Shanghai, Eula told me she wanted to visit her son, who was living in Boston. Tsu-Ming arranged for this, even buying her an airline ticket to the United States and helping her obtain a passport and visa on short notice. It took a lot of effort. We flew back to the United States together, and I remember that on the flight Eula slipped the airline's high-quality, stainless steel flatware into her large pocketbook. I was dismayed, and told her, "You cannot take that. You are stealing airline property." She ignored me and kept the silverware.

Eula stayed in our home for three weeks. Her visit was difficult. She was a chain-smoker, and after promising Tsu-Ming she would not smoke in our house, she did so anyway. Eula also seemed unimpressed by our hospitality. We took her to visit the Mackinac Bridge, and to see Copper Harbor, an area known for its beautiful vistas of Lake Superior and the north woods. She surprised me by saying, "We have more beautiful places in China." Once, we argued violently. She threatened to pack up and leave, but couldn't because she did not speak English. "How are you going to leave? Who is going to take you?" I asked. I was exasperated and called Tsu-Ming, who came home from work and talked with Eula to calm her down.

Eula and I traveled to visit friends in Valparaiso, Indiana, for a few days. After our visit, one of those friends asked me what Eula had been like at my home. I said she had been difficult, and that nothing seemed to please her. "She told me she didn't have enough to eat at your house," said my friend. "And that she bought a gift for her son that you took for yourself." I was shocked. This was absolutely untrue. Eula had given me an ornament intricately carved from ox horn, saying it was a gift. Yet, here I was being accused of stealing it. As for the complaint about the food, after finishing the meals we served her, Eula refused to eat more, despite multiple urgings for her to partake further. It was a complete surprise to hear of her dissatisfaction. My friend reassured me, saying, "We didn't believe what she told us about you. We know you, and never believed what she said about you."

Still, I felt hurt and wanted no reminder of this person. I put the ornament on the floor, stomped it to pieces, and burned all Eula's letters in the fireplace. Later, Eula wrote me a letter, but I did not reply. Then she called and asked if I had received the letter. When I told her I had, she wanted to know why I had not answered. "I don't want anything to do with you," I said. "Don't contact me again." I remember that my mother was visiting us at the time, and said, "You did the right thing." I was happy that I never heard from Eula again.

It became clear to me that since being hospitalized together as young women in Shanghai, Eula and I had grown up in very different environments, and that our ways of thinking had also grown to be very different. For instance, during the Cultural Revolution resources became limited, and as a result, family and personal relationships—long an important part of the social fabric of Chinese society—had been degraded. Eula had learned the concept of *guanxi*, or "connection," a mode of social interaction in which favors are exchanged among people to achieve one's goals. It seemed to me that, in Eula's mind, *guanxi* had taken priority over any cultivation of friendship between us. She saw me only as someone who had become useful to her.

12   The Mining Journal, Marquette, Mich.

Fri June 16, 19

Top Research Post Given Han By CCI

ISHPEMING — Announcement was made today by Dr. S. W. Sundeen, manager of research and ore development

CHINESE GEOLOGIST—Doing microscopic work in Ishpeming this summer for the Cleveland-Cliffs Iron Co. is Tsu Ming home is in Honan province in China. Han, a graduate stu University of Minnesota, has not heard from his family in the Communists took control of the Chinese mainland.— Homburg).

S. W. Sundeen, manager of re

Young Chinese Geologist On CCI Job In Ishpeming

ISHPEMING, July 1—A young Chinese geologist, employed here for the summer by the Cleveland-Cliffs Iron Co., has become a "man without a country" since

ceiving his doctorate if munists are still in c the country.

But if it becomes no

Fossil found in U.P. one of world's oldest

Mine find tops 2 billion years

MILWAUKEE SENTINEL   Monday, April 5. 1993

Lansing, Mich. —AP— It was soft and squiggly, a kind of prehistoric pond scum that might have inspired an insult or two among rival cave men.

No bones about it, remains of an algae-like organism found en-

support this kind of life," said Han, a Chinese immigrant who recently retired as a senior research scientist for Cleveland-Cliffs Mining Co. in Empire.

Han first found signs of the fossil in 1974, when a routine

198

Chapter 22
SAD, BITTERSWEET YEARS

As the children grew up, Tsu-Ming traveled more and more, going to different cities in the United States or to foreign countries to attend professional meetings where he presented papers. While the children were still living at home, I did not go with him. Later, I accompanied him to places such as Salt Lake City and Phoenix. We also took trips to London, Paris, Norway, and Belgium, where we visited some relatives from Taiwan. I really enjoyed all our travels together, and these trips—which were a lot of fun—helped balance out the more serious, and sometimes difficult, times in our marriage.

In 2001, two of my closest high school friends, Esther Chen and Deling Xie, came from California, where they lived, to visit me. On October 10, we celebrated the Chinese holiday of Double Ten Day, which commemorates the founding of the Republic of China in 1911. We stayed overnight in a motel in St. Ignace, Michigan, at the northern end of the Mackinac Bridge, where we ate moon cakes, round Chinese pastries filled with lotus seed paste and egg yolk that Esther and Deling had brought from San Francisco's Chinatown. That night there was a full moon and we were inspired to write a four-line poem in the traditional Chinese style.

Tsu-Ming retired in 1992 at the age of sixty-eight, after forty years at Cleveland-Cliffs. He had moved up through the ranks to become a senior research scientist, and was considered an expert in his field. He also discovered, through fieldwork at the Empire Mine in Negaunee, Michigan, what was then the oldest fossil in the world visible to the naked eye, *Grypania* cf. *spiralis*. Because the fossil was determined to be 700 million to 1,000 million years older than similar fossils found in Montana, China, and India, the discovery provided evidence that complex life forms (eukaryotes) existed earlier in geologic history than previously thought. "Curiosity was and still is the driving force for me to conduct my research," Tsu-Ming told an interviewer in 1993. I know he also was grateful for the respect he earned from his colleagues.

Tsu-Ming had always been a hard worker, often putting in long hours even

憂情，苦樂雜陳的歲月

Opposite foreground: This photo was taken as Tsu-Ming emerged from the Tilden Mine in Ishpeming sometime in the 1980s after collecting pellet samples.

Opposite background: Tsu-Ming's work generated some publicity, especially after his discovery of an ancient fossil in 1993.

Tsu-Ming and I enjoyed traveling together. Here we are on a trip to Norway in 1996.

when on vacation. In fact, one of his coworkers said he always knew when Tsu-Ming was on vacation because he came to work at eight thirty in the morning instead of eight o'clock. This was because he loved his work! After his retirement, Cleveland-Cliffs gave Tsu-Ming an office so he could continue to work on his own schedule. However, he still kept his usual hours; at his retirement party, a colleague who was paying tribute to Tsu-Ming said that the only thing different about Tsu-Ming after he retired was that he came to the lab in his tennis shoes instead of dressy shoes!

In 1999, the Institute on Lake Superior Geology awarded Tsu-Ming its Goldich Medal for his work solving geological problems. He was also honored by the Michigan Iron Industry Museum. Russell M. Magnaghi and James F. Shefchik, in their book, *Tsu-Ming Han: Man of Two Different Worlds,* describe Tsu-Ming as an "incredible scientist" and "one of the most prominent Chinese American immigrants" to settle in Michigan. They credit him with playing "an important role in the sustainability of an entire community and an industry having a direct impact on the lives and fortunes [of] thousands of people in this outer rim of the United States." The book was published in 2016 by Northern Michigan University's Center for Upper Peninsula Studies. Tsu-Ming's papers are held in the center's archives.

Yet despite his professional success, Tsu-Ming experienced years of depression, the result of two lifelong regrets. One was failing to complete his PhD at the University of Minnesota. Unlike me, he had not studied English growing up, and as a result, his spoken English wasn't strong enough to pass his oral exam. The fact that English was not Tsu-Ming's native language, however, was something that his professors refused to take into consideration. His other big regret was losing contact with his family for so many years, something, of course, he was unable to control.

I retired at the end of March 1994, just before Easter, but the beginning of my retirement turned out to be quite traumatic. Tsu-Ming and I had planned to celebrate the Easter Season with Dennis and his family in Milwaukee, and then visit my parents in College Park. On the same trip, Tsu-Ming had arranged to meet with a Japanese professor, Dr. Iwasaki, who was working at the US Geological Survey in Reston, Virginia. My sister, Lois, was also visiting my parents, and on our way to pick up Tsu-Ming after his meeting, we noticed a great commotion just outside Dr. Iwasaki's office. There was Tsu-Ming, lying on the floor writhing in great pain, with a doctor in a white coat bending over him. It was a very frightening sight! The doctor ruled out a heart attack, but had Tsu-Ming taken to Reston Hospital Center, where after what seemed like hours of waiting we were told that the doctors detected an aortic aneurysm, a weakened area in a section of Tsu-Ming's aorta, the body's main artery, and arranged for Tsu-Ming to be airlifted to Inova Fairfax Hospital.

While waiting for the helicopter, Lois and I prayed. Psalm 46: 1, 2, 4, and 10 really comforted and calmed me. At Fairfax

Hospital, doctors diagnosed the problem as a descending aortic dissection, a fissure between the aorta and its inner lining. They believed it had been caused by high blood pressure and did not recommend surgery. Tsu-Ming was heavily sedated, but by the next morning was awake and in no pain. I was very thankful. Tsu-Ming stayed in the Cardiovascular Intensive Care Unit for nearly two weeks, on blood pressure medication and under close observation before we flew to Milwaukee, where Dennis had made an appointment for his father to see a cardiothoracic surgeon. Eventually, the decision was made to continue treating the dissection with medication and careful blood pressure monitoring.

In 1995, after Tsu-Ming's health had stabilized, I started volunteering at the local Salvation Army, an organization I have held in high regard all my life. I first learned about the Salvation Army when I was a little girl in China during World War II. I knew their volunteers helped people in distress, and remember that we were given food during the most difficult years of the war. My young mind was greatly impressed by the good works they did and I thanked God for their help. In Ishpeming, I was put in the office doing paperwork and other odd jobs. I really enjoyed both the work and meeting new people. Over the years,

I also visited the residents of local nursing homes, served lunch at apartments for senior citizens, and operated a coffee cart at Bell Memorial. My volunteer work brought me much pleasure, and reminded me of the many blessings I had enjoyed.

The following year I also joined a singing group! Our group consisted of six ladies: five Finnish and one Chinese. We sang mostly Christian songs in both English and Finnish. Miss Anna Kulju, a retired schoolteacher, was our leader. Three ladies played the guitar, and two played the autoharp. I considered myself a "living music stand," because I held the sheet music for my friend Marie Rogers.

We sang from 1996 to 2005, in churches, senior centers, and at a few other events such as wedding anniversaries and funerals. Several summers we also sang in the Marquette Scandinavian Midsummer Festival in Presque Isle Park on the shore of beautiful Lake Superior. We became known as the No Name Group because we could never come up with a name!

An exciting opportunity arose for us when we were invited to appear on a local Finnish television program, *Finland Calling*. The program ran for fifty-three years, hosted the entire time by Carl Pellonpaa, a record in TV broadcasting. Carl gave each of us a video recording of the

In 1996 I joined a local singing group. We performed in churches, senior centers, and at local events. Here we are putting on a program at Concordia Lutheran Church in Palmer, Michigan.

program so we could enjoy looking at and listening to ourselves.

One time we were invited to sing in a senior apartment building in Ishpeming. When we got there, we saw a flyer on the bulletin board at the entrance announcing that the afternoon's program would be presented by The Heavenly Tones. We thought there had been a mix-up, or that we were there on the wrong date. But we found out that was the name the organizers had given us.

Tragedy struck my family in October 1998, when Samuel, who was living in Timonium, Maryland, was injured in a car accident shortly after he retired. His spinal cord was severed and he was paralyzed from the neck down. He lived a little over a year and died in January 2000, at the age of sixty-five. It was a terrible time for all of us, and particularly my mother, who had to endure watching her firstborn son suffer and die. I went to stay with my sister-in-law Rosie three times to help her take care of Samuel before he passed away, and saw him again the day before he died, staying until after his death. Rosie, who was from Canada, returned there later in the year for a family reunion and died suddenly. So, both Samuel and Rosie died in the same year. That was very difficult for their two children.

Our familiy (left to right: me, Tim, my mother, Dennis, and Tsu-Ming) celebrated my mother's one hundredth birthday in June 2003. She lived almost five more years without any serious health problems. Lisa couldn't attend because she was living in China.

CCI scientist remembered as mining pioneer

By JACQUELINE PERRY
Journal Ishpeming Bureau

ISHPEMING -- A former Cleveland-Cliffs Inc. senior research scientist responsible for developing a mining process that has dominated the North American iron ore industry for more than 50 years has died.

Tsu-Ming Han, who helped develop and improve the current iron ore pelletizing and concentration process, died Thursday at his Ishpeming home. He was 80 years old.

"He was one of the people who pioneered and continuously refined the pelletizing and concentration operations used in the iron ore industry through his microscopic studies of iron ore and pellets," said Cliffs spokesman Dale Hemmila.

"He was a tireless research scientist and a extremely likeable person."

Han was born Sept. 11, 1924 in China's Henan Province. He came to the United States in 1948 to earn his master's degree in geology from the University of Cincinnati. He earned a master's in economic geology in 1952 from the University of Minnesota. He became a citizen in 1961.

Han joined Cliffs in April 1953 as a mineralogist at the company's research laboratory in Ishpeming. He was the first mineralogist hired at Cleveland-Cliffs to evaluate low-grade iron ores at the Humboldt, Republic, Empire, Tilden, North Lake, and Cascade mines, according to information provided by the Michigan Iron Industry Museum. Han was later promoted to senior research scientist, a position he held until his 1993 retirement from Cliffs.

Han is survived by his wife, Joy; sons Dennis and Timothy; daughter, Lisa; one brother, two sisters, and seven grandchildren.

Funeral services will be at 2:30 p.m. Sunday at Calvary Baptist Church in Negaunee. He will be interred in Graceland Cemetery in Milwaukee.

HAN

Tsu-Ming's obituary highlighted his very successful career at Cleveland-Cliffs.

In 2002, Tsu-Ming was treated for an ulcer, but when his health got worse, Dennis advised us to go to the Mayo Clinic in Rochester, Minnesota. There, Tsu-Ming was diagnosed with stomach cancer and underwent surgery. I found a room to rent nearby, and Dennis and Tim both came to visit. Our pastor from Ishpeming, Randy Reed, drove through the night to be with us the day of surgery, for which I was very grateful. After a few days Tsu-Ming was discharged. I drove all the way home, only the second time I had ever driven for more than three hundred miles.

Tsu-Ming recovered, and lived three more years before passing away on February 3, 2005, at the age of eighty-one. By then we had been married more than forty-eight years. Lisa and her family, and Tsu-Ming's younger sister, had come from China for a visit shortly before he passed away, but had to return a few days before his death.

Tsu-Ming was so well known and so highly respected that about two hundred people, including some from out of town, came to his funeral at our church, Calvary Baptist. I received many sympathy cards, and members of my church family prepared and delivered meals to my home for about two weeks. I was very thankful. Our local newspaper, the *Mining Journal*, published Tsu-Ming's obituary, headlined "CCI scientist remembered as mining pioneer." In the article, which noted Tsu-Ming's work in refining the pelletizing and concentration process for the iron ore industry, he was described as a "tireless research scientist and extremely likeable person." Shortly after Tsu-Ming's funeral, Lois came from Florida to stay with me for three weeks. While she was here, I had time to write more than two hundred thank-you notes.

After Tsu-Ming's death I felt terribly alone, but I decided to stay in our house, where I still live after all these years. I had no desire to move because I had such good neighbors, many longtime friends, and my church, which was very important to me.

My mother died in March 2008, at the age of 104 and without any serious health problems. After my father's death in 1985, she lived with Lois in Ocala for a year before returning to the home where she and my father had lived in College Park. Later, she lived for a while with each of her three youngest sons, and spent several summers with me in Ishpeming, where she loved the perfect weather.

EPILOGUE

尾
語

When I reflect upon my life, I some-times find it hard to believe all that I have seen and experienced. I will never forget the delightful, carefree hours I spent grow-ing silkworms, milking my grandmother's goats, and playing in the South Tree Pavil-ion as a child; the three wonderful years I enjoyed at Mary Hardin-Baylor College; and the happy family life I enjoyed with Tsu-Ming and our children in Ishpeming. But I also witnessed terrible, world-altering events, including Pearl Harbor Day and the fall of Shanghai; was devastated when diagnosed with tuberculosis at the age of sixteen; and watched in sadness and with great anxiety as my mother struggled, on her own, to keep our family together while her world was crumbling around her.

My mother, in fact, is one of the two peo-ple in my life who influenced me the most. I remember her as both a near-perfect wife and the best mother in the world. I never heard her raise her voice or argue with my father, setting a good example for her children. And as a mother, she was strong, resourceful, and very patient. She also was always willing to help people in need, and I remember her bagging up food and clothing for those less fortunate than we were. What a remarkable life she had.

The second person was my Auntie Zemma, who showed me and my siblings so much love, and taught us a great deal about many interesting things, including America. I was only ten years old when she returned to the United States for cancer treatment, and we never saw her again. But by then she had already put me on the path to attending her alma mater, Mary Hardin-Baylor College, a life-changing experience.

The most difficult time in my life was in 1950 when at the age of nineteen I found myself living on my own in Hong Kong and preparing to leave for America. I really didn't want to go. I had always been a shy and quiet young girl who was scared of strangers and strange places, and I was afraid of what lay ahead. I had no idea of what I would find in the United States, and feared that my English was not ade-quate. Of course, emigrating to America was absolutely the right thing to do, and I feel blessed to be a US citizen.

I am thankful for my parents, shown here in 1969.

Overall, I feel very grateful for all that God has given me. I was raised by Christian parents who brought me up in the Word of God. I received a good education, enjoyed a long, interesting career and a happy marriage, and was blessed with three wonderful children. I am so glad that they are well educated and happy, and so grateful for my five grandchildren, who are all quite accomplished in their chosen pursuits.

I don't have too many regrets about my life. I should have studied harder and made better grades so my father would have been more pleased with me. Looking back, I now realize that he was very strict with us, perhaps because as an important leader in the church and the principal of a school, he felt his children should always do the best of all. I also know now that although he was highly respected, he also was feared by many who knew him. (One of my cousins told me that as a child even she had always been afraid of him!) Another regret is that I didn't persist in teaching my children Chinese, instead giving in to their pleas to play with their friends after school.

The most important lesson I have learned in life is to trust in God, who blessed and protected me many times over the years. I often wonder why God spared my life, and delivered me, my parents, and my siblings out of Communist China to America. I now believe that the trials and tribulations I encountered—growing up in China during a time of great upheaval, coming down with tuberculosis, enduring the deaths of my husband, brother, and friends—all happened to make me stronger and to learn to empathize with those suffering similar difficulties.

I thank God for leading me in my life and for all the people He sent my way to help and guide me in my life's journey.

REFERENCES

Clark, Carl A. n.d. *Who Walk in Faith: The Saga of the Peter H. Lee Family*. Silver Spring, MD: The True Light Book Room.

Han, Tsu-Ming. 2004. "Autobiography of Tsu-Ming Han: Life Journey of a Chinese Country Boy." Unpublished manuscript in the Tsu-Ming Han papers, MSS-296, Central Upper Peninsula and Northern Michigan University Archives, Northern Michigan University.

Holmes, David B., and Wenben Yaun. 2008. *Chinese Milwaukee*. Charleston, SC: Arcadia Publishing.

Magnaghi, Russell M., and James F. Shefchik. 2016. *Tsu-Ming Han: Man of Two Different Worlds*. Marquette, MI: Center for Upper Peninsula Studies, Northern Michigan University.

Morton, W. Scott, and Charlton M. Lewis. 2005. *China: Its History and Culture*. 4th ed. New York: McGraw-Hill Inc.